What people are saying about Kiril Sokoloff's *Personal Transformation:*

Each time I read this book, it's as though I'm reading it for the first time. Each experience Kiril speaks of brings new meaning to my soul...A great book...*I've learned so much, not just about hearing and not hearing, but about life...For so many people with the same handicap but also for people in general*...Courageous, open, genuine, and honest...*This book is a "must" for friends and spouses of hearing-impaired persons to gain a better understanding of what they can do to improve communication*...Transforms suffering into joy and love...*Kiril's book will be an inspiration for everyone who reads it...* Touches the human spirit on many levels...*Powerful and direct!*...I can't wait to share it with so many people...*Made me cry*...Never read anything like this in my life...*So grateful to receive the gift of this journey*...Marvelous book...*First rate*...Everything you wanted to know about deafness but were afraid to ask...*Superb*...It brought tears to my eyes...*It made me really think about things I may take lightly*...It was beautiful...*This story about personal fear and courage has left an indelible impression*...Magnificent!!! It provides a simple and incredibly graceful empathy...*Destined to be a best seller*...Once I started reading it I could do nothing until I finished it...*I am crying and I cannot stop...tears of joy and sadness.* Kiril's book will make a lot of people cry...and for all good reasons...*Just being human is a monstrous challenge. It takes such suffering to open our hearts to ourselves and each other* ... Thank you for Kiril's heroic struggle, thank you for going to the depths of the loneliness, thank you for taking the time to write about it. Kiril has taken this journey for all of us... *What a terrific and courageous story!* ... Love has the power to heal all wounds and erase all sorrow... *This book reads like one of my truly favorite authors — Dostoevsky* ... This book has the potential to be life-transforming for many people: I don't mean simply by increasing sensitivity to late-life deafness, but also by sharing insights into living a good life... *Kiril tells his story so eloquently and with such honesty. I have been in tears several times* ... His writing has put me closer in touch with my feelings... *Kiril has taught me so much* ... Extraordinary on so many dimensions: beautifully written and totally honest... *Reminds us all to count our blessings, of which we have many, each and every day* ... The book's intensity kept me reading into the wee hours last night... *The story is wonderful. It needs to be told* ... Fine writing. Intelligent, poignant, and sensitive. This book can provide much comfort to those who are lonely or who have had to endure the pain of separation from loved ones... *From the beginning up to the end, I couldn't stop reading it... Really quite marvelous. I cried all the way through it!* ... I'm, quite simply, awed by the honest, courageous way Kiril related his story... Thank you for sharing this immensely wonderful epiphany... *Kiril's eloquent and unexpectedly staccato style is so compelling* ... I can't begin to say how this book touched my heart. I couldn't put it down until I had read every word. Many people will experience a healing when they read this book... *To me the book was more than a book about being deaf. It was the adventure of a courageous man overcoming adversity. I hope that if I ever have to face such a challenge, I will do as well...* The book touched me deeply... *This book is fantastic* ... This story is inspirational... *I felt healed...* There is a sort of a raw, emotional impact one gets from reading the book. This is a very personal property written with great compassion ... *Enlightening, moving, provoking, and exquisitely insightful...* Wonderful to read such a human story... *We realize we are not alone in our journeys...* Kiril's spirit of courage and undaunted determination... has turned iron ore into gold... *A poignant memoir, sure to touch people's hearts and make them more aware of our daily efforts, struggles, and embarrassments* ... This book gave me much greater understanding and appreciation of the magnitude of being deaf. I am grateful for this new awareness... *What struck me was how Kiril turned a handicap into an asset...* This book will be so helpful to so many people, and so enlightening to so many people... *I thank Kiril for educating me, for raising my sense of awareness. I simply never imagined the frustrations nor the loneliness.*

This is an amazing story,
full of truth and hardship, full of compassion and hope,
full of the beauty that resides within all people of disabilities
(and when you think about it, don't we all have some?).

PERSONAL
TRANSFORMATION

PERSONAL TRANSFORMATION

An Executive's Story of
Struggle and Spiritual
Awakening

—————————————

KIRIL SOKOLOFF

WITH
FOREWORD BY
HIS HOLINESS THE
DALAI LAMA

A Crossroad Book
The Crossroad Publishing Company
New York

The Crossroad Publishing Company
16 Penn Plaza, Suite 1550, New York, NY 10001

Printed in the United States of America

This text of this book is set in 10.5/13 Sabon. The display font is Universe.

Library of Congress Cataloging-in-Publication Data
Sokoloff, Kiril.
    Personal transformation : an executive's story of struggle and spiritual awakening / Kiril Sokoloff ; with a foreword by His Holiness the Dalai Lama.
      p. cm.
    Includes bibliographical references.
    ISBN 0-8245-2299-0 (alk. paper)
    1. Sokoloff, Kiril. 2. Spiritual biography. 3. Deafness – Religious aspects. 4. Self-actualization (Psychology) – Religious aspects I. Title.
BL73.S63A3 2005
305.9′082′092 – dc22

                         2005014779

1 2 3 4 5 6 7 8 9 10   10 09 08 07 06 05

How I Learned to Love Myself, Open My Heart,
and Surrender to the Will of the Universe

For All the Lonely People
Whoever You Are, Wherever You Are

As long as space endures, as long as sentient beings remain, until then, may I too remain and dispel the miseries of the world.

—His Holiness the Dalai Lama

For me there can be no relaxation with my fellow men, no refined conversations, no mutual exchange of ideas. I must live almost alone, like one who has been banished. I can mix with society only as much as true necessity demands. If I approach near to people a hot terror seizes upon me, and I fear being exposed to the danger that my condition might be noticed....

But what a humiliation for me when someone standing next to me heard a flute in the distance and I heard nothing, or someone standing next to me heard a shepherd singing and again I heard nothing. Such incidents drove me almost to despair.

—Ludwig Van Beethoven

Illness is the doctor to whom we pay most heed: to kindness, to knowledge we make promises only: pain we obey.

—Marcel Proust

The most terrible disease that can ever strike a human being is to have no one near him to be loved. Without a heart full of love, without generous hands, it is impossible to cure a man suffering of loneliness.
—Mother Teresa

Contents

THE DALAI LAMA

FOREWORD

I believe that the purpose of our lives is to achieve happiness. But happiness is of two kinds: one that derives from physical comfort, and the other that essentially flows from our minds and our thoughts. Of these two, the happiness that derives from the mind is the more important. If we maintain a positive attitude and our mind is calm and happy, we can put up with discomfort and physical challenges. Sensual pleasure alone will never set the mind at ease. When our minds are restless and disturbed no amount of luxury or physical comfort can make us happy.

This gives rise to the question – can we transform our attitudes? The Tibetan Buddhist tradition preserves simple but far-reaching techniques for training the mind, particularly dealing with concern for others and turning adversity to advantage. These have virtually become part of the Tibetan character. I believe it is this pattern of thought, transforming problems into happiness that has enabled the Tibetan people to maintain their dignity and spirit in the face of great difficulties. Indeed, I have found this advice of great practical benefit in my own life.

In this book, *Personal Transformation*, Kiril Sokoloff tells how he has come to terms with late deafness, an affliction that severely impairs the ability to communicate with other people. In doing so he demonstrates the power of developing a positive attitude and refusing to accept defeat, which I am sure will be a source of strength and inspiration to many readers.

Introduction

*I am resolved on an undertaking that has no model and will
have no imitator. I want to show my fellow-men a man in
all the truth of nature; and this man is to be myself.*

— Jean-Jacques Rousseau, *Confessions*

ELEN KELLER was blind and deaf. She said, "The blind are
cut off from things and the deaf are cut off from people."
Most people think it's worse to be blind than deaf. But how
would they know?

Voltaire once wrote that he didn't have the time to write
a short letter, so he wrote a long one instead. This is my attempt to write a "short letter" — on deafness. It's also about
losing my precious hearing, how I fought back, found meaning
in my suffering, accepted fate, turned negatives to positives, grew
spiritually, and learned to love life as never before.

Mine is not a particularly sad or noteworthy tale. Walk down
the street one block or knock on the apartment door next to
you, and there is always someone who has it worse.

In the early 1980s, I interviewed dozens of late-deafened
adults. I have spent time with many others since. There are
reportedly nearly 30 million Americans with a hearing impair-
ment, a figure that will rise steadily as the baby boomers age.
Many millions more are children, grandchildren, spouses, or
friends of late-deafened adults, all of whom are anxious to learn
how best to communicate with us.

Our world is different from that of people who are born deaf,
"sign," and live almost exclusively in an all-deaf environment.
Late-deafened adults were born into the hearing world and that's

where their friends, family, and business and social connections remain. That's where they hope to stay.

This book is my story. I can't speak for other deaf people, but I can tell you about my experience. It's the story I know best.

It is difficult, I assure you, to open old wounds and write of subjects that I have never discussed with anyone. I've never liked talking about myself or my handicap. I am afraid that my revelations — of fears, weaknesses, sadness, and loneliness — will cause people to think less of me.

At some point in our lives we all experience loss. Our parents, relatives, or friends pass away suddenly. We lose our faculties. We age. Life is one loss after another. How you handle loss says a lot about what kind of person you are.

I have found that deep wounds, hidden suffering, loneliness, and sadness are pervasive — even in the "happiest" of families. Many people are searching for something, whether it's love, truth, a healing of their pain, someone to understand them, or even one friend who loves them unconditionally. "If I show the real me will anyone like me? Am I lovable for myself alone?"

These words are rarely said: "I truly know how you feel. I'm lonely too. I have this great grief that I can't talk to anyone about. I'm so afraid, so lonely, so sad, so depressed! I want to believe in something. People betrayed me. My faith is gone, and I can't trust anymore. I don't want any more pain. Will you hold me, protect me, and tell me you love me? Please, can you comfort me?"

We think our sorrows and wounds are unique until we find other people with similar afflictions. But then we discover this: I'm alone. She's lonely. He has hidden sorrows he can't talk about. We are connected through our suffering — and in finding each other, we join a community.

Deafness gave me many precious gifts. I developed an acute intuition. Forced to become a bystander, I learned powerful skills of observation. Through suffering, loneliness, and despair, I grew as a human being, and I found compassion on a large scale. Conquering the challenge of deafness, I traveled on a long journey of my soul. I released anger and stress. I learned to love myself, to open my heart, and to surrender to the will of the universe. I also found peace of mind and empowerment.

I've written this book about my journey for the lonely people and those burdened with sorrows, sadness, and pain. It is my devout wish that this book may offer them a healing.

Durch Leiden Freude.

Joy through sorrow.

1

What I Don't Hear

IF YOU HAVE a strong imagination, you can try to visualize the life of a handicapped person. Close your eyes and stumble around the room, feeling the wall for direction. Or sit in a wheelchair and think of life without ever walking again. But deafness is a handicap that is harder to imagine. Putting cotton in your ears for an hour tells you little about the affliction. Essentially, deafness is about failure at the most basic and fundamental level of human interaction — communication.

Let me begin this book by telling you what I don't hear. I miss the intonation and pitch of voices, the emphasis on words, the meaning of silences, the nuances in the way words are delivered. I don't hear the names of people to whom I am introduced, no matter how many times I ask them to repeat. Words in a sentence have a context, but people's names don't. I don't understand foreigners with heavy accents, particularly the Chinese and the British. I don't hear the spoken words of children. I can't hear in a crowded room with background noise.

I can't comprehend the waiter when he tells me about the specials and asks what kind of salad dressing I want, how I want my meat cooked, what type of vegetables or potatoes I would like. I can't understand conversation in a movie or on a videocassette unless it is subtitled or has closed captions. I can't hear what they ask me at passport control. I don't know what the clerk at the airport check-in is asking. I never hear a word tour guides say. I do not understand a word of lectures or speeches, particularly if there is a microphone.

17

I can't follow conversation if the lighting is poor. I can't understand what people say who have mustaches or beards. I can't hear people who don't enunciate. I can't follow people who speak quickly and nervously. I do not understand people who mumble and don't move their lips. I cannot understand people who speak with their hands in front of their mouths. Conversing on airplanes is very difficult because the roar of the engine drowns out all sound of speech.

I am unable to eat *and* talk. I am unable to walk *and* talk. I cannot follow a conversation when a person does not face me when he or she speaks. I cannot hear when more than one person speaks at the same time. I cannot follow speech in a noisy restaurant. (All restaurants are noisy, despite people's efforts to find quiet ones.) Rooms with poor acoustics, where voices echo, are the most difficult places for me to carry on a conversation.

I can't hear a word spoken in a room with background music or a piano player. I cannot hear loudspeaker announcements of any kind. I don't know I'm being addressed if someone is behind me, for example, in an elevator. I do not hear when people talk to me from afar, shout from another room, or speak when walking in front of me.

I am unable to understand what my lover says at night in bed with the lights off. I can't hear alarm clocks. I do not comprehend speech when people are farther than five feet away from me. I can't follow what people are saying who whisper in my ear. (They often whisper in the wrong ear and I need to read lips.) If you are talking to a group, and you turn away from me, I won't hear you. I don't "listen" to music anymore. At best, it's like attempting to feel the softness of silk or the texture of velvet through thick work gloves.

Hearing aids are extremely sensitive to moisture. A small amount of water or sweat can damage $6,000 hearing aids. So hearing-impaired people can't wear hearing aids at the gym, during sports, or when it's raining. We can't hear you during those times.

I can drive *and* listen, although it sometimes terrifies people the way I do it. I adjust the rear view mirror so I can see the lips of the person sitting next to or behind me. I turn on the interior light and read their lips while driving. It's been successful for over fifteen years. Please don't tell the police in my area.

People who know me well look at my eyes. Does he understand? Other friends make me repeat what is said — did I hear? The reality is that I comprehend very little, if anything, of group conversation or one-on-one conversations in crowded, noisy rooms.

The goal of a deaf person is to make the appropriate non-committal facial responses — and hope that while you are smiling, someone isn't talking about a personal tragedy. Frequently, conversations change three or four times before I know it. If I interject a comment on a subject that was discarded five minutes ago, I feel stupid, so I usually keep mum.

Every day I interact with people, and conversation requires an effort. By the end of the day, I am exhausted. Many deaf people retreat rather than go through this. The real skill is to figure out when a question is coming. Luckily, most people like to talk. Few people ask questions. There is often a lift in someone's speech or the eyebrows rise, if a question is asked. If I study carefully, more often than not I can guess that I'm heading for the hot seat.

Participating in the social and hearing world takes special effort. Sometimes, someone will ask me a question, and no matter how many times I ask for repetitions, I still can't understand. Other times, I am fearful that by maintaining the same facial expression in a long conversation, I am not responding appropriately to what I am told. If I interfere with the free flow of conversation, it grinds to a halt. If people stop frequently to repeat, spontaneity is lost. Besides, they won't do it for long or, worse, they'll avoid me, or so we deaf believe.

I'm frequently asked, "Why don't you tell people you aren't hearing them?" The reality is that many people are incapable of changing their speech patterns. Here's a typical answer when you tell someone you are deaf: "Oh, yes, I also have a hearing problem in my left ear." What they mean is they have a mild high-frequency loss. They hear fine. They'll speak up for about one minute before reverting to their prior way of speaking.

So, if some people won't change, you must do what I do. Participate by osmosis. Laugh when people laugh, smile when they smile, be serious when they are serious. Later, you find out what happened. That is, *if* your spouse or companion is a good listener, cares to chronicle what happened, and is patient enough to answer all your questions.

Or, alternatively, you can turn a handicap into an asset. You lose one of your senses, you gain another. In my case, my intuition grew and grew. It's my most valuable asset. I have insights into people that I never had when I heard well.

2

The Stress of Deafness

Research suggests that loneliness may affect not merely the perception of pain but actual bodily health. Those who live alone have premature death rates at least double the national average. Among divorced people, the suicide rate is five times higher, and the fatal accident rate four times higher. Married cancer patients live longer than unmarried cancer patients.

—Philip Yancey and Dr. Paul Brand, *The Gift of Pain*

THE LESS I HEAR, the more stress. Sometimes, I am so tense I can't look people in the eye. Since I am lip-reading, eye contact is difficult anyway. I wonder nervously if the person thinks I am weird, timid, or fearful because I avoid eye contact. Women are particularly uncomfortable with men who are unable to make eye contact. Also, after lip-reading for a period of time, it's hard to break the habit, even when the circumstances are optimal for hearing.

I'm on an airplane. We are sitting on the runway. The pilot makes an announcement. I watch people's faces — they are angry and upset.

"What's the problem?" Of course, I have no idea.

I'm invited to a dinner party where I don't know anyone. The acoustics are terrible. The conversation echoes, and every sound is magnified, so voices are impossible to comprehend. The lighting is low — romantic, the way most people like it. Not only am I unable to hear a word that is spoken, I'm also unable to lip-read because of inadequate lighting. Because I know no one, I feel incredibly isolated and alone. I'm terrified someone will start asking me questions, with the other guests witnessing my humiliation.

I'm in a long line at a deli for my morning coffee and Danish. The checkout man is a foreigner with a heavy accent and a huge mustache. I can't hear him when he says the price. I ask him to repeat. He shouts the answer. His body language is very angry and negative. He looks at me as if I am stupid. I resolve forever after to pay with a large bill, so this won't occur again. But the incident grates on me for weeks.

I'm alone in my house. I still have some speech recognition. My car has mechanical problems and I am unable to drive to a scheduled tennis match. There's not much time. I call information for my partner's phone number. I listen to the recorded announcement and write down the number. There is no way, with my phone system at the time, to connect directly to the number.

I dial.

It's the wrong number.

I repeat the process.

Wrong number.

I repeat the process.

Wrong number.

I repeat the process.

Wrong number.

And so on.

I finally reach the point that for the first time in my life I want to tear the cord out of the socket and hurl the phone across the room.

I have an important meeting in Boston that I *cannot* miss. I must catch the 6:30 a.m. shuttle from LaGuardia Airport, a fifty-minute drive from my house. The deaf don't hear alarm clocks. The "wake-up" vibrator under the pillow doesn't work for me. I'm afraid it might fall off the bed in the middle of the night. I have a lamp by my bed that flickers on and off when the phone rings. This is my alarm clock. My associate calls at 5:00 a.m., but I am so tired, the flickering light does not wake me. The light flashes for forty-five minutes before I awake. I have forty-five minutes to dress and get to the airport. The stress is unbelievable. But I make it with thirty seconds to spare. Forever after, I am never able to sleep when I have to rise early.

Loneliness. I dedicate this book to all the lonely people. It took years for me to get over loneliness — not that I hung on to it, but the cumulative loneliness took a long, long time to work off. I'm a voracious reader. I love books and reading and the knowledge and intellectual stimulus they bring. A good book can keep you from feeling alone.

But occasionally, I panic. If someone cancels an invitation for dinner and I'm faced with an evening alone, I'm consumed with a raw terror — even now, years after I went deaf. I know it's unnatural and stupid. Most times, I can deal with it, but sometimes I can't. The weekends are particularly horrible if I'm alone. Even the *prospect* of spending a weekend or Saturday night or Sunday by myself causes me great stress.

"Why don't you remarry so you won't be alone?" they ask.

"Loneliness isn't a valid reason for marriage," I answer. "You also have to be in love."

I'm on a two-week business trip around the world with a friend. We are visiting Korea, Japan, Vietnam, Cambodia, and India. I've taken a large number of hearing aid batteries. For some reason, they quickly wear out. I have only a few left. We are in Hanoi, with still a week left of travel and important meetings ahead of us. I panic. Will my batteries last? Can we find replacements in a place like Hanoi? Luckily, our guide is able to locate the model I use and replenish my inventory. Who would think that something so small as a battery for a hearing aid could cause such stress?

If you think running out of batteries is stressful, consider actually losing the hearing aid, which I do from time to time, if only temporarily. It almost always happens immediately before a social event — when you need it most. A working hearing aid is your lifeline to the world.

I find it very stressful to be without sound. As soon as I've finished taking a shower I can't wait to put the hearing aid back on. While I look for the lost hearing aid, my blood pressure nearly boils. Consider the simple act of waiting in a high-rise building for the elevator. Because I don't hear the bing of the elevator's arrival, I must turn my head to the front and back, front and back, front and back, to catch the blinking light before the elevator door closes on me. If I am in a hurry, miss a few opportunities, and the elevators are busy, I can be delayed for some time, my blood pressure rising all the while. Who would ever imagine there could be stress in getting on an elevator?

Deafness puts a huge strain on a marriage. The hearing partner carries an enormous burden. I'm a realist on the subject. I know how much work it takes. I look at the effort and sometimes wonder whether I'm worth it. I'm not talking about self-worth. I'm merely addressing the issue of effort and patience. I'm not talking about a visit to the dentist's chair that is over in an hour. Deafness is a permanent state and requires a long-term, ongoing effort. I find myself wondering, again and again, whether the burden of this friendship, or this relationship, is too great to be sustained for long. Perhaps, this is the ultimate stress of deafness. At least it is for me.

3

The Invisible Handicap

WHY DON'T YOU carry a large sign around your neck that reads, "I'm deaf"? It's not as insensitive or impractical a question as it might seem at first. Many years ago, when I still had most of my hearing, I stopped at a liquor store in the Murray Hill area of Manhattan. The proprietor had two very visible hearing aids. We started talking about hearing loss. "I don't have batteries in these hearing aids," he said. "The aids don't work for me, but I wear them to remind people or to make them aware that I'm hearing impaired."

When I bought my first hearing aids, the technology wasn't as advanced as it is today. They made a plastic mold that fit very tightly in my ear canal — to concentrate the power of the hearing aid. The mold was connected to the hearing aid with a two-inch plastic wire, and the hearing aid fit over the back of my ear. These were very visible hearing aids, yet few people saw them. Nowadays, most people wear such tiny hearing aids that unless someone shows you, they aren't noticeable. When women's hair covers their ears, it is virtually impossible to know they are wearing hearing aids.

Other handicaps, of course, are highly visible and easily recognizable. There is no question in anyone's mind when a man or woman is blind or paralyzed. The hearing-impaired, on the other hand, usually try to hide their hearing aids and their deafness. There is a reason for this, which may be the most grossly misunderstood part of the life of late-deafened adults. Deaf and *dumb*. The saddest discovery for a late-deafened adult is that

25

many people still believe it's true. Dumb, of course, in this expression means mute, not stupid. But to many people, deaf is stupid.

It's hard enough to adjust to the slow or rapid death of sound and music and the human voice, but to be considered stupid is more than some of us can bear. Since deafness is an invisible handicap, and we often do not respond, or we answer incorrectly, the speaker becomes irritated and thinks we are rude or stupid. In a supermarket, when a hearing woman is behind me in line and says, "Excuse me," and I don't move, her first thought is not that I can't hear, but that I purposely am mean and inconsiderate. This leads to a complex issue: people see the world through their own experience, which limits their ability to understand life from another person's point of view.

People who are not hearing impaired have difficulty adjusting to deafness because it makes them feel foolish. They are uncomfortable repeating, rephrasing, and speaking slowly. It's as if *they* are doing something wrong. As if *they* are the "problem." They would rather be seen as the "solution" — the one who helps the blind person cross the street. When they help the blind or weak, they see themselves in a positive light. They are performing an act of kindness that others can appreciate. If, however, they have to repeat what they say several times, they become very self-conscious because in some way the focus has become negative rather than positive. This is why deafness remains such a chronically mistreated handicap and why late-deafened adults retreat from the world. A hearing-impaired friend says, "No one can imagine the energy we expend to hear or how we *pretend* to hear to be accepted as 'normal.'"

The hearing world also sees lipreading and hearing aids as solutions to deafness. They are not. Unfortunately, lipreading has severe limitations. Silently mouth the following three words while looking into the mirror: "man," "bad," and "pat." You'll notice they all look alike. Say the word, "Harry." You will see the H's are impossible to lip-read. If these and other similar words are key words in a sentence, it is easy to misread what the person is saying. Unless you are flexible enough to make the changes in your brain quickly (it can't be "man," so it must be "pat"), and most people aren't, the task becomes so draining that almost everyone gives up and withdraws from conversation. Even the very best lip-reader comprehends only 70 to 75 percent under optimal conditions. Poor lighting, lack of lip movement, facial hair, sounds that can't be lip-read, faces that are turned away from you, rapid-fire conversation in a large group, people who talk with their hands in front of their mouths, heavy accents, talking heads that bob up and down and are visually hard to follow — all these render lipreading impossible or exceedingly difficult.

Hearing aids are as frustrating as they are helpful. They amplify everything, not just voices. The blowing of the wind, background conversation, knives and forks clattering on plates, water pouring into a glass, a car's engine, airplane exhaust — all are extremely loud, and, unfortunately, louder than speech.

4

The Joke's on Me

THERE'S A LIGHT SIDE to deafness. We often hear incorrectly, and the results can be hilarious. It's my birthday. A friend takes me out to dinner, and later, to a nightclub, which is filled with gorgeous women, provocatively dressed. One of the women approaches me. The nightclub is dark and very noisy. She asks me a question. It's too noisy and dark to have a chance of hearing, so I say, "Yes." I usually say yes when I'm asked questions that I don't hear. She begins to dance in front of me, or, more precisely, six inches away from me. After a few minutes, she stops dancing. She asks me another question.

Again, I say, "Yes." She dances again. Another question, more dancing, and so on for twenty minutes.

Then she puts her face right next to mine and I *do* hear: "You owe me two hundred dollars."

I laugh, point to my friend, and say, "It's my birthday! He's paying."

Another time, I'm giving a presentation at a client's office in Boston. I'm sitting at a very long table. A man at the opposite end asks a question. I'm nearsighted, in addition to being deaf. I cannot hear his voice, and I can barely see his lips. I launch into a ten-minute answer about the prospects for the dollar. I find out later he asked me about the Chinese economy.

I'm flying to Miami for the weekend to meet a friend. I'm recently single. A very pretty flight attendant smiles at me and asks me a question. I ask her to repeat. You can't say "what?"

or "excuse me?" to a pretty woman more than once. Take my word for it.

I still don't hear, so I say, "No." Her face clouds in anger, and the man sitting next to me gives me a strange look. The flight attendant won't look at me or talk to me for the rest of the flight. I never learned what she asked me, but that's about the time I started answering "yes" to all questions.

Often, I cannot distinguish between a man's and a woman's voice on the phone. I call a friend's house. Lucy answers the phone, and I say, "Hi, Bob." Bob answers the phone, and I say, "Hi, Lucy."

My assistant is out sick one day, and I answer the phone. The voice is friendly, but I have no idea who it is. Three times I say, "I'm sorry, it's a bad connection, I can't hear who this is."

It's hopeless. I don't recognize the voice, and I can't hear the name. So I fake it. "Oh, hi!" I say. The friend speaks for a few minutes. It's all mumbo-jumbo. Later, I'm at the gym. The same friend comes up to me and says, "Great! You are here. I didn't think you understood me earlier."

I'm at Gigi's, a popular bar in Boca Raton. I'm sitting on a bar stool next to my friend Bob, each of us puffing on a long cigar. A very attractive woman walks by, speaks to me, takes my cigar, puffs on it, and then sticks it back in my mouth and leaves. I look at Bob and ask, "What did she say?"

He repeats the answer three times. By the time I understand, the woman has vanished. Here's what she said: "Mind if I suck on your cigar?"

When I work out, I don't wear a hearing aid because it can get damaged by the slightest amount of moisture. So in the gym I'm totally deaf. A man working out next to me says a few words. I don't know whether he is speaking to me or to my trainer. I figure it must be the latter. I turn and walk to the next station. My trainer walks over to me, with a big smile on his face. He says, "Jack never says anything nice about anyone. But he said you are really making a lot of progress. And then you ignored

him, turned your back, and walked away." I apologize profusely
to Jack, and we all have a good laugh.

Fred lives in San Francisco, despite his fear of earthquakes.
On the very early morning news, I hear there are tremors in
California. It's 2:00 a.m., but I call Fred anyway; he may need
reassurance. A young girl answers the phone and says, "Hello,
hello...hello...HELLO!" This is definitely not his fiancé, so I
end the call.

The next day Fred calls me. He says, "Why did you call me
last night and hang up. I've got caller ID, and I saw it was you."

"I was embarrassed because a strange girl answered the
phone."

"That was *me*," says Fred.

I use a special hairbrush that vibrates to stimulate growth of
the hair follicles. Sometimes the switch goes on automatically,
creating a frightening noise, depending on where it is at the time.
Several times it has gone off as I'm about to go through airport
security. Other times, it starts to vibrate in my bathroom drawer.
I hear this shattering reverberation, but I've no idea where it is
coming from, or what is causing it. Often, I have to seek someone's help to locate the source of the sound, and I'm always
relieved that the solution is as simple as turning off a switch.

Mishaps like this are a frequent part of my life, and I laugh
at them. So do others.

You can't take yourself too seriously in this world, particularly
if you are deaf. I don't. How can I, when so many outrageous,
funny, and ridiculous things happen to me?

5

My Russian Soul

But beware: to conquer a fortress one must first conquer one's own soul. —Milorad Pavic, *Dictionary of the Khazars*

P ROBABLY THE MOST PROFOUND experience of my young life occurred on my tenth birthday. I don't particularly like birthday parties now, and I liked them even less then. Nevertheless, my mother encouraged me to have the first big birthday party of my life. All my young friends were invited to our home. My father, who had a severe stuttering problem, told my mother that he would absent himself to spare me the embarrassment of his affliction. This was the day I learned about my Russian soul.

My father was a refugee from the Russian Revolution, born in St. Petersburg. He was without a country for many years, and every time he passed through customs anywhere in the world he became so nervous that I still feel his stress and pain. He left Russia with almost no possessions.

My father grew up as a member of the old Russian intelligentsia, who were well known for their idealism. Poverty was something to be proud of, a conviction almost as powerful as the Buddhist vow of poverty. My father was the only person I ever met who never wanted to impress anyone. I never saw him lose his temper in all the years I knew him. He was a fervent believer in democratic ideals and was a member of the Social Revolutionary Party. He was a prodigy of sorts, graduating from medical school while a young teenager. My father came to this country in the late 1920s at the invitation of the Rockefeller Institute. Later, he worked at Columbia University and with the famous cancer scientist Dr. Leo Loeb at Washington University in St. Louis.

English was my father's third or fourth language, which he learned in his late thirties, and he struggled with it his whole life. His speech impediment was less severe when he spoke French or Russian. Nevertheless, in a classic triumph over adversity, my father wrote twenty-seven books in English, with my mother responsible for the heavy grammatical editing on all of his written work.

My father was a member of the All-Russian Constituent Assembly during the brief period of democracy after the overthrow of the czar and the coming to power of the Bolsheviks. Lenin, and later Stalin, successfully bamboozled the West with socialist propaganda. My father always believed the Communists were totally unscrupulous and would stop at nothing to achieve world domination. He presented this view in books, articles, letters to politicians, and editorials in local and national newspapers. He never gave up, and I wish he had lived to see the fall of Communism in 1989.

My father was a very accomplished scientist with a Ph.D. and a patent for bioflavenoids. He was way ahead of his time in many ways. Beginning in the 1940s, he became a fervent believer in the power of bioflavenoids, vitamin C, a low-fat diet, no salt or sugar, many small meals a day, and exercise. He spent almost his entire life looking for a cancer cure, literally up until the day he died. My father never talked to me about his life in Russia or our family. I learned what I know from his books.

St. Petersburg has an unusual history. My father wrote two books about its unique character. St. Petersburg is called the "Venice of the North" and since its founding has been the cultural and intellectual center of Russia. It is one of the most spiritual cities in the world. During World War II, when it was known as Leningrad, it was surrounded by German troops for nearly three years. Stalin viewed the city as a hotbed of "liberal sentiment" and would have been happy to see it crushed. It survived only because of the spirit of its people, who refused to capitulate to either Hitler or Stalin.

On a trip to St. Petersburg (in 1991, after the fall of Communism, it reverted to its old name) in the fall of 1999, I had a direct experience of the passion of that commitment. I was traveling with a group of friends, and our tour guide was a short Russian woman of five feet three inches and a true resident of St. Petersburg in every sense of the word.

One of the participants asked her whether the outcome for St. Petersburg would have been different if Hitler had invaded Russia in the spring instead of the late summer. She responded with one of the most passionate soliloquies I have ever heard. She said that over one million people were evacuated from the city during World War II across Lake Ladoga in heroic circumstances, and another million died of starvation, bombing, and artillery fire. Stalin wanted the city to die, but the people of the city, feeling responsible for the preservation of the cultural heritage of Russia, refused to let it happen. She told us about the suffering and commitment and passion of the people, and when she finished talking, no one in our group said a word for thirty minutes.

My first visit to St. Petersburg was one of the most moving experiences of my life. I walked down the streets where Dostoevsky's characters walked, visited the apartment where my father had lived, saw the university where he conducted had his scientific research, watched the flowing of the River Neva. I felt like I had come home, and of course I had.

Dostoevsky is a uniquely Russian author. He wrote eloquently about the Russian soul, and by the time I was twelve I had read all his books, some many times. *Crime and Punishment* is his best-known and most popular book in the West. There is a scene in *Crime and Punishment* that, in my opinion, provides great insight into the Russian soul. Raskolnikov, the book's protagonist, has murdered a pawnbroker to commit the perfect crime. But later his guilt consumes him and he seeks absolution.

He suddenly recalled Sonia's words. "Go to the cross-
roads, bow down to the people, kiss the earth, for you have
sinned against it too, and say aloud to the whole world, 'I
am a murderer.' " . . . He knelt down in the middle of the
square, bowed down to the earth, and kissed that filthy
earth with bliss and rapture. He got up and bowed down
a second time.

Dostoevsky believed that growth comes through suffering. If
everything in your life is positive, you don't ask the questions or
learn the truths that are the catalyst for growth. It is only adversity that makes you question who you are, how you must change,
and what you need to learn. There are many variations on this
theme. Suffering deepens and awakens the soul. Suffering height-
ens sensitivity. Suffering leads to spiritual development. Suffering
makes you know what's really important. Suffering teaches you
compassion for others. Suffering teaches you to forgive yourself
and to open your heart. Suffering makes you appreciate what
you have, not what you miss or think you want. Suffering raises
your consciousness, so you feel more deeply than before and see
beauty everywhere.

The Russian soul is deep. It feels pain and beauty profoundly
and therefore has a great capacity for suffering and spiritual
growth. My earliest memories were thinking about the meaning
of life, the goal of the universe. What was *my* purpose, if any?
For most of my young years I questioned whether anything I did
had any real meaning. No matter what I attempted, I questioned
its relevance. When I was seven or eight years old I realized
material possessions were ephemeral.

Sasha Migunov is a Russian writer of several successful novels
who was born in St. Petersburg and now lives in Florida. He
believes that there is no universal truth — only the search for
it. Russians like Sasha and myself debate such subjects all night
long. We are always obsessively searching for truth, "the truth."

The major story of the first thirty years of my life was acute
self-consciousness. I hated it, despised being a constant prisoner

to my concern about what people thought. I knew better, but I couldn't help myself. My father said that my self-consciousness was due to an inferiority complex. I wished it away a thousand times, willed it away a million times. But fate held me firmly in its grasp.

I came into this world with a great sense of unworthiness, or so my Chinese feng shui masters said after looking up my birth date in the *Book of Destiny* and studying my astrological chart. The core lesson for me in life was to overcome those feelings and learn to trust a higher power to protect myself. When I could do this, the feng shui masters said, I would begin to show my true self to the world and, as I traveled along the innocent path, serve as an inspiration to others.

Even before I fully understood this, I knew intuitively that you get what you need in life, not what you want. What I needed was a spiritual journey and the development of my Russian soul. That's what happened, and I thank God for it every day.

6

My Deafness Gene

Of all these cracks in the building, the only one that affected the soul—and that terribly—was, as we know, the deafness. —Romain Rolland, *Beethoven the Creator*

I HAVE A DEAFNESS GENE. Most deafness is genetic—in other words, preordained. My paternal grandmother was deaf, so I had a 25 percent chance of going deaf. Pretty good odds, until you know the wild card; my father was over sixty when I was born. Steve Jones in *The Language of Genes* points out that "there are more chances for things to go wrong in men (who—unlike women—produce their sex cells throughout life, rather than making a store of them at puberty)." The older the father, the greater the chance of passing along the bad gene. In this case, the odds rose to a 100 percent certainty of deafness.

I learned all this long after the fact. My father never told me of my grandmother's deafness. Both my parents had excellent hearing, so I assumed my loss was environmental rather than genetic.

Between 1918 and 1992, my family inside Russia had no contact with those family members living outside. If you were known to have a relative outside Russia, the Communists sent you to Siberia, to a "comfortable dacha" at the edge of the Arctic Circle where you became a slave laborer if you lived long enough. When I first visited St. Petersburg, I found that my father's sister—long deceased—had such a terrible stuttering problem that she was forced to drop out of medical school.

My father's stuttering problem, as devastating as it was, apparently was less severe than hers, because he successfully graduated from university and medical school. In an ironic twist of fate, my father was a very powerful orator. He was well known in Russia for his inflammatory speeches about democratic ideals. However, an audience of one or a few was hard for him.

Clearly, I inherited a neurological disorder that plagued other family members. Would it have made a difference if my father told me my grandmother was deaf? Would I have run my life differently? As genetic testing becomes the order of the day, more people will face this question: Do you want to know your genetic blueprint? I am one of the people who wants to know. If your life will be short, better to find out while you still have the time to treasure every moment.

In my case, I took a lot of preemptive steps — long before I became deaf. Would I have taken more preemptive steps? Would the anxiety of impending deafness have increased the level of my stress and fear? It's hard to know the answer, and the question is moot anyway.

As I ponder my struggle with deafness, I imagine the pain my father's sister must have gone through. I watched my father struggle to talk with the outside world. I never saw my father use a telephone, deal with a tradesman, or verbally defend himself against an insult. How did he feel about being so helpless and vulnerable? I often wondered what it was like to serve on the Russian front in World War I, as my father did, to see the horrors of the Russian Civil War, the dreams of democracy crushed by the Bolsheviks, to lose your country, to leave behind your family, friends, and possessions, to start over in a new country with no money and a new language, to encounter all this with the stress of a huge stuttering problem, to have no connections in the new world you were entering, to watch your prediction of the communist horrors come true as Stalin murdered tens of millions and destroyed the Russian fiber for a generation, to see Hitler kill an estimated 30 million of your compatriots (and no one should be fooled, it was Russia that broke the back of Hitler's army) —

and never say a word about it to your family and loved ones. What did he do to survive immigration — the dozens of times he encountered it, with no passport, no money, and a stuttering problem probably out of control with stress? I put my deafness next to him, and I am mightily humbled.

I heard my father talk only once about his speech impediment, when one day, late in life, he told me he should have put more effort into curing it. I have heard stories of how people have overcome severe stuttering. I know it can be done, but perhaps not in every case. Maybe the neurological dysfunction is such that for some people there is no cure. I often wonder what was going on in my father's mind as he tensed up when he struggled to communicate with someone.

Tension was pervasive in my family when I grew up. Did stuttering cause tension, or did tension cause stuttering, or did they reinforce one another? Stuttering probably put my father's nervous system under huge stress — similar to what I have experienced with deafness. I wish I had had the compassion at the time to look for ways to reduce my father's stress. As I think of him, gone these many years, my heart fills with love and compassion for his gentleness, kindness, and suffering. I wish I could hold his hand and tell him that I love him *for* his stuttering and suffering. I want to hug him tenderly.

"Please come to my birthday party! I am so proud of you. You need not talk to my ten-year-old friends. Be yourself and they will love you, as I do. It's all right, Pafi, I will take care of you. Don't worry! Let me carry the burdens of your worries. Let me take on the pain of your suffering." I didn't say it then, but I know he hears me now and rejoices in my Russian soul. He accomplished a lot, and I am very proud of him, but I wish I had helped him more. It's too late for me — but perhaps not for you.

I can honestly say that never once in my life did the thought cross my mind that I wished for a different set of genes. My father was a great man, and I am privileged to be his son.

7

What Made Me Who I Am

MY FATHER almost never gave me advice. But when he did, I never forgot it. When I was sixteen he said, "Kiril, a *man* keeps his word to himself." It was a long time before I fully understood what he meant. I've tried to explain it to people for years, and I hope I have finally found the formula. Keeping your word to yourself is not about self-discipline, although that comes with the territory. What it means to me is that you can't keep your word to others unless you keep it to yourself first. It's only then that you can go on to keep your commitments to others.

My mother came from a long line of doctors. The first one graduated from the University of Pennsylvania Medical School in 1788. In a direct line, through my grandfather, every single one was a doctor. My grandfather was head of neurology at Columbia University and was considered one of the greatest neurologists of the twentieth century.

I'll tell you two stories about my mother's upbringing, and from that you can gather the effect on me, albeit a generation later. When my uncle was ten years old, he broke a window on the family farm and lied about it. My grandfather congregated the farm staff, and in front of them and my uncle said, "My son is a liar." At dinner that night, as the story goes, rather than being antagonistic or withdrawn, my uncle nestled up to my grandfather. I can tell you this: my uncle had more integrity than any other man I ever met.

The other story involves my mother. When she was twelve years old she fell off her horse and broke her collarbone. My grandfather made her saddle the horse — by herself — and ride twice around the paddock.

A few years ago my mother fell and broke her hip. She was forced to remain in her bathroom on the floor for hours before someone came to find her. Due to her many medications, the ambulance staff decided it was risky to give her any painkillers until she reached the hospital. The ambulance driver — after he drove her two hours to the nearest hospital — said she never complained, cried, or said a word. The bouncing of the ambulance causes intense pain to those injured in this way. "I've taken a lot of other men and women to the hospital with similar injuries, and, even with some painkillers, they all screamed," he said.

My mother is a remarkable woman, the equal of my father in many ways. She, too, came from an unusual background. Her mother, Alice Nolan, was reportedly one of the most beautiful women in the world. I have a portrait of her in my home, and I can attest to the fact. She resembles a more lovely, more vulnerable Princess Diana, with a haunting sadness and helplessness that no doubt broke a hundred hearts in her era.

Alice's father launched her on an unusual path. Where is the best French spoken? Go there and learn French. The best German? The best Italian? By the time she was eighteen, she spoke four languages like a native and had the culture that went with it. She died when I was fifteen, but I was her favorite grandson, and she spent many summers reading me Shakespeare and telling me imaginary stories that went on for weeks. She had an incredible presence. I imagine all very beautiful women do, and if they know how to use that presence they can turn the world upside down. And she seemed to when I was around her.

I never knew my grandfather. He died of cancer years before I was born. But he won my grandmother, which no doubt was a major accomplishment, as she had dozens of suitors from all over Europe and the United States. She delayed marriage until she was in her thirties, which in her generation was almost unheard of, the ultimate testimony to her beauty and the full range of her choices. My grandfather won the race by always being around but never flattering her. Men unwisely think that the way to a beautiful woman's heart is compliments. It's simply not true, particularly if you are only part of a huge chorus.

My mother grew up in New York City and on the family farm, about an hour north of the city. Like my father, she was a prodigy of sorts, graduating from high school at age fifteen, but she was a victim of the Depression and had to leave college at the end of her first year.

My mother had an amazing career; she was an extraordinarily gifted pianist. She composed music that was performed at Carnegie Hall, and for twenty-five years she wrote a newspaper column reviewing classical music. She wrote three biographies of famous women, and, of course, she dealt with my father's stuttering problem for thirty-two years. My father said she was a world-class pianist who was too shy to perform in public.

One great-grandfather on my mother's side was Irish, and my mother claimed to have inherited a powerful intuition from the "old country." My uncle said her premonitions were never right, but my own experience was that she was rarely wrong. She sized people up, saw into their characters, knew how they would behave, judged correctly whether they were trustworthy, forecasted impending trouble time and again, understood personal strengths and weaknesses, and saw the flaws in marriages and relationships. My feng shui masters said that in a prior life she belonged to a family of kings and queens, not hard to believe. You can call her vision an incredible judgment or intuition or a combination of both. Luckily, I inherited some of this skill, and whatever I inherited was augmented through deafness.

My mother believes that if little things go right, it's a good omen. This is another way of saying that it was meant to be. My mother inculcated this attitude in me at an early age. When small positives occurred at major turning points in my life, or as I was making an important choice, I had the confidence to plunge ahead. And she was right, the small successes led to big ones.

I was an only child, and I had a very unusual upbringing. For years I was ashamed of being an only child, perhaps because it implies I never learned to share, but more probably because I was so sensitive about my loneliness. My mother, father, and I constantly worried that I would develop a stuttering problem. This is an amusing confirmation of the old truth that the problems you worry about never occur; it's the ones you *don't* worry about that bring you to your knees.

I was acutely sensitive from a young age. My mother reports she picked me up at a nursery one day when I was three years old, and I was crying because I'd seen an older boy hurt a young, defenseless one. For many years, even battle-hardened as I now am, a friend could criticize me harshly and push me into a brief depression. All the wishing in the world never made me less sensitive. At the right time, when my defenses were down a "friend" could do some serious damage.

Rejection of any kind hurt me profoundly. I can remember many small incidents that seem absurd, but caused me great pain: not being invited to a party when others were, sitting alone at the dining table at school and hoping some of my classmates would join me (they rarely did, preferring to sit with the popular boys), seeing others receive constant phone calls when no one called me. My distress undoubtedly stemmed from my inferiority complex. Being aware of the cause did nothing to ease my fears surrounding rejection and indeed actually increased my self-loathing for worrying about such shallow matters.

I became an expert at emotional camouflage. I also knew who I could trust with my feelings: no one. Nevertheless, I was full of excitement; it's my nature to be passionate about life. But my mother said no to so many things that my youthful enthusiasm was squashed, and I was wounded profoundly. I let go of that pain, however, many years ago.

I was also painfully shy. My mother told me that shyness inevitably yields its rewards — the joy of heightened sensitivity. It took many years for my shyness to go away, and for many years I questioned the rewards relative to the pain of getting there, but no longer. I was also very spiritual. I remember praying for everyone in my life, world peace, and world happiness, starting at the age of five. Until I was a young teenager, I was so filled with love for my parents that I prayed every night that we would all live to the same age.

Between the ages of eight and seventeen, I spent every other summer in Europe with my parents. By the time I was twelve, I had seen every major museum, cathedral, and palace in Europe. I knew Paris, London, Venice, Florence, Athens, Rome, Vienna, and Geneva. By the time I was sixteen, I had either read or seen all of the major Shakespearean plays. I grew up with classical music in the house and was emotionally involved with all the great composers for most of my young life. I read many of the world's greatest writers, and books became my unconditional friends who never disappointed.

My parents lived a highly individualistic life. They spoke French together in the United States and English in Europe so their conversation would be private. When my parents left New York for Florida, they rented by mail a house that they had never seen and subsequently lived in it for almost thirty years. My mother hated the house, as well as Florida, expecting each year to be their last. But my father liked the warm weather. My mother was never emotionally involved in either the house or Florida, so I never felt like I had any roots until I went to college.

Traveling with my parents was very lonely for me as a young boy. We stayed at hotels in London, Paris, Nice, Geneva, and Ascona on Lago Maggiore in Switzerland. There were rarely any young children at these hotels, and the ones I befriended always left soon afterward. My major sport at the time was table tennis. I can still remember my sadness at the age of twelve when a pretty German girl, with whom I played ping-pong every day, suddenly had to depart, leaving me with a huge void.

I occupied my time by reading. The rule in our family was that there were unlimited funds to buy books. At the beginning of every summer we visited several of the great London bookstores, and I bought fifty or more books for the summer. I love books. They have rescued me from loneliness countless times. If I had to give everything else up in my material life, I would choose to hold on to my books till the end. But books can't replace the childhood I never had. I remember being desperate for companions for most of my young years. As I reminisce about those times, a sadness comes over me. They say you can't be a good writer unless you've had a lonely childhood. Mark one up for my writing career.

I went away to boarding school when I was eleven. My mother wanted me to have the best possible education, which I received, but at a price that may have been too steep. I went to a school that squashed independent thinking, creativity, and originality. Conform or die! I suppose I should be grateful for learning survival lessons in a cruel community. Many of the boys were sarcastic, while the teachers turned a blind eye and lived in an ivory tower. Nevertheless, I "prospered" — if you can call it that — in the environment, but I lost touch with my Russian soul and my spirituality, although I didn't have the time or the knowledge to worry about it then.

Afterward I went to Georgetown University to major in languages. But the deafness gene was already working on me. After the first year, I was not able to keep up with the intensive language training because I couldn't hear the sounds. My grades in Russian fell from a straight A to B to C to D. I knew I had to change my major, which I did reluctantly at the end of my sophomore year. By the time I graduated from college at twenty-one, I had a superb education, a certain amount of self-discipline, a very wide view of the world through my travels and family background, a rich cultural heritage, an insatiable curiosity about life, a great pent-up loneliness, as well as a major inferiority complex.

I began work immediately after college in New York City. But trouble began almost at once as deafness pressed in on me. I had a choice. Fight with everything I had or give up. When late-deafened adults are faced with deafness, most of them withdraw. The challenges are simply more than the spirit can bear. But I chose a different path. I resolved not to withdraw. I promised myself I would try to do everything that a hearing person does — no matter how painful, stressful, or difficult. I could participate, I told myself, through intuition, reading body language, looking at people's eyes, and studying their character.

You never know what you are made of until you have been really tested, failed, hit bottom (you think), staggered to your feet again, only to be thrown to the floor again, and again, and again. Deafness made me who I am. Deafness pushed me down — below the waterline many times — molded me, toughened me and softened me, shaped my character and the way I look at life. I will never know what kind of person I would have been had I never lost my hearing, but I can tell you I would not be the man I am today.

8

My Double Calamity

───────────────
═══════════════
─────────

MY MARRIAGE ended in 1988. I went totally deaf in my good
ear in the same year. A double loss. People liken divorce
to a death, and it is. A double death. Your friends desert you,
your social life collapses, and people avoid you like the plague.
Your friends should stand by you in a divorce, but only a few do,
and the betrayal is so great that you need to make a whole new
set of friends. I never take sides, and as a result of my experience
I'll move heaven and earth to help a divorced friend of either sex
in need, no questions asked!

I separated from my wife, Kati, after twelve years of marriage.
To her credit, my deafness had nothing to do with our breakup.
A wife who truly loves you offers you so much nurturing that
it eases the pain and isolation of those entering the deaf world.
At the very time I needed it most, I lost that nurturing. So as
I grieved for my lost hearing, I also grieved for my lost wife
and the breakup of my family. Any problems facing children
are magnified in a divorced household. You blame yourself for
bad grades or trouble at school, and even the littlest things that
go wrong are somehow blown up in your mind to tragic and
enormous proportions.

Kati was brought up in Mexico of American parents, and she
had a sweetness and enthusiasm that touched me deeply, especially compared to tough and hardened New York women. I
proposed six weeks after meeting her, and we were married two
months later, a "long delay" only because the parents needed

time to orchestrate a big wedding. I doubt there are many married couples who had more fun at their wedding.

Yet our marriage was troubled from the start. Many years later, one of Kati's therapists told me she was manic-depressive, which made her hypersensitive. The smallest incident would set off a chain reaction. She subconsciously attributed her depression to me, or so he said, which made her angry, and she punished me by retreating into an icy-cold isolation for days. I kept a diary of her withdrawals and bad moods, and later, when I showed it to her, she could not believe how much of the time she spent in depression. This went on for many years.

Constant withdrawal by someone who loves you is very hurtful. She withdrew from me so often it became an integral part of our lives. I think of her withdrawal as a dagger thrust into the heart of our marriage.

Nevertheless, I loved her deeply and, in her own way, she loved me profoundly, although her dependency on me might be viewed as unnatural. The more dependent she became on me, the more responsible for her I felt — to the point that, as our marriage ended, it was agony for me to turn her loose unprotected, as I saw it then. My mother thought Kati's helplessness was my Achilles heel. Her weakness and dependency attracted me to her, and my strength and determination attracted her to me.

She had a tough childhood with little nurturing. She attended a junior college in Boston, and her father made her pay for her own tickets to fly back to Mexico. Christmas was very important to Kati and was a big event in her family. In order to pay for her tickets, Kati gave foot rubs to rich, spoiled girls, no doubt a humbling experience. When I married her, she had one dress to her name.

As I look back, I realize she had very low self-esteem. An early picture from our first year of marriage shows her eyes shyly averted, unable to look at the camera. Perhaps Kati's mother, Anne, set the pattern. At our first meeting, Anne was unable to make eye contact with me even once during the entire dinner. A marriage counselor once described Kati as a sack that couldn't stand up unless you were holding it. Another said, "She's like a glass with no bottom. You pour and pour and pour. It never fills, and no matter how much support you give her, it's never enough." Maybe that was too harsh, but there is some truth to it.

When we were married, she occasionally gave tutoring lessons in Spanish. She was a good teacher and, of course, spoke impeccable Spanish. The tutoring was a source of pride to her. One day, she met two businessmen who wanted some Spanish tutoring before a trip to Latin America. She offered to meet with them in New York City. They invited her to lunch on Wall Street, which was almost a four-hour round-trip commute. She traveled all the way to the appointed meeting, but they didn't show up and never called to explain or apologize. I grieved for years at the way she was treated, and it says a lot about our relationship and my feelings for her. I couldn't bear for her to be hurt, and I tried in every way possible to help with her depression and to support her emotionally. It never entered my mind that marriage was a two-way street — that I could actually receive emotional support as well.

Of course, the Mexico that she was brought up in was different in culture and lifestyle. That compounded her dependency. I did literally everything for her, and it is only with the passing of time that I can admit how deeply frustrating it was. Nevertheless, I felt a bond of responsibility to take care of her that I'm sure many people would see as ridiculous. But that's the way I felt and the way I behaved.

It took me years to get over the sadness of the end of our marriage. I was a living example of hanging on to grief and guilt for way too long. What hurt most — after our separation — was her sadness and helplessness, and that I was no longer there for her, although I was supportive in many ways up until only a few years ago. It's easy to see in retrospect how one should let those feelings go, but it's hard to do. I had a seven-year mourning period. Going deaf and the grief of the breakup of my family was nothing next to the pain I suffered for her. One day someone will fully explain it to me. In the meantime, I'll offer a few explanations. I felt responsible for her in a way that a parent is responsible for a child, but in some ways it was even deeper than that. The more I understood her emotional problems, the greater obligation I felt to personally help her. I also loved her.

She was very funny and silly, a wonderful contrast to my intensity and seriousness. She made me laugh, and to this day, my children and I laugh over some of the things she did. She reached me in a very special place — my inner soul — and I felt as if I had an infinite compassion for her troubles, her depressions, her weaknesses, and the insensitivities to her by her family members. In some ways, the more unstable she became, the more I loved her. And then I broke her heart by ending the marriage, making her fend for herself, steeling my heart to her needs — to save myself.

We lived in a house that had been in my family for several generations. My wife understood the family attachment and gracefully insisted that I stay in the house. I bought her a house a few miles away. The day she moved out was the saddest day — up to that point — in both of our lives. She picked me up in the late afternoon and drove me to her new house and showed me how it looked. She tried to be excited about the new furniture and the way she had decorated the house, but both of us were so consumed with grief that, try as we could, we were unable to hide the sadness from each other.

When she drove me home, it began raining very heavily. She came inside for a few minutes — to the house where we had lived for ten years as a married couple with joy, happiness, and fun — and then, sadly, it was time to go. She opened the door and began walking in the rain to the car. The light was on at the back door and I could see her frail shoulders hunched against the rain. I wanted to call after her: "Don't go! Come back! I love you!" But I couldn't and didn't, and so closed a chapter of my life. Then I learned what loneliness was really about. I thought I knew this subject from my childhood, but the universe had a big surprise for me — a *real* test of the limits of my endurance.

I learned what it was like to live in a house that had been full of joy and now was dark and lifeless. I learned what it was like to feel like the last person left alive in the universe. I couldn't make or receive telephone calls. I had no friends left in the community. I missed my children with a longing that actually caused me physical pain. I will never forget leaving the office during those years. There was a long wait at the local stoplight. It lasted for three and sometimes five minutes. I sat there night after night, dreading going home, fearing the night and the darkness, and I would bend over with a physical pain in my stomach like an ulcer.

When the children were not with me, the house was frighteningly empty. You could feel the sadness and grief in the house. It was palpable, like a heavy humidity dripping down the walls and windows. At the time, I lived in northern Westchester County, about an hour from New York City. This was a rural area, and at night I could not see my neighbors' lights. There is something about light at night that helps keep away despair and loneliness. Darkness is simply that — darkness. Driving up to a house at night without any lights on is very depressing, particularly if it was once filled with the lights and activities of your family.

There was a small apartment over the garage on my property. I rented it to a young man who also helped with odd chores around the property. The first night he moved in, I looked out my window, saw his lights on, and my heart leaped with joy. Such a small event, but it brought me such happiness. There is someone here. I'm not alone!

9

My Children,
My Heart

MY HEART BEGAN to really open when I had my first child, my son, Jay. I never knew such love. I can understand how a husband feels neglected by his wife when a baby arrives. I had such a strong love for Jay that I kissed him and hugged him dozens of times a day. I was present at his birth, and he screamed with such agony that I will never forget it — or ever want to see its like again. I came to understand the Hindu concept that we arrive on earth with total innocence and that the trauma of birth is so severe we never regain it.

When Jay was about two years old, after he arrived home from the day-care center he would climb the stairs to my little office and sit quietly on my lap for hours as I worked. He couldn't bear to be away from me, nor I from him.

My daughter, Emily, by contrast, never cried when she was born. Later, in the nursery, I saw a nurse scrubbing her down, with Emily fighting and kicking her off. I always wanted a daughter, even more than a son. My father died before my daughter was born, which is truly sad, because the men in our family always had a weakness for their daughters and grand-daughters. Emily was not a beautiful baby. We actually worried that she might not be very pretty. It's ironic, because she is now a world-class beauty who doesn't know it, and I think she'll be lucky enough to never find out.

As her birth experience suggested, Emily has enormous re-
silience and strength. She also has a lot of determination. A story
from her young childhood will illustrate my point. Emily loves
art, and she was very devoted to her coloring books. We took
the children to Washington to visit my in-laws. On the entire
trip from New York, Emily worked passionately on a coloring
book. Emily continued to work on her coloring book all through
dinner and well into the night — until we turned the light off so
she had to stop. I awoke with the first light of day, and there was
Emily diligently completing her coloring book. I love her deeply
for her strength and for the positive spin she puts on everything.
My daughter walks into any room and the lights go on. She's
full of happiness and joy. I've never seen her unhappy, angry, or
depressed. She is an inspiration to all of us.

My son, my son. My dear, dear son, my dearest son. How I
love you. If only I could explain to you, dear reader, the great
compassion and love I have for my son. When I separated from
my wife, she wisely and kindly agreed to joint parenting because
I don't think I could have survived being parted from him at that
time. During his early years, I couldn't bear to take a business
trip, or even spend one night away, I loved him so much.

Two examples: My son is not yet two years old. My daughter
is yet to be born. We go out to dinner. After we take the babysit-
ter home, I go into my son's room and watch him sleeping, then
take him into my arms, carry him into our bedroom, and put
him to sleep on my chest, hugging him to me with all the love in
my heart.

It's bedtime. My wife puts Jay to bed. She sings him a lullaby;
we call it "cuckoo" in our family. She sings and sings and sings.
He is still wide awake and not yet ready for sleep. Then, he
says, "Daddy, cuckoo! Daddy, cuckoo! Daddy, cuckoo!" I enter
the bedroom, kiss him, hold him in my arms, and sing, "Daddy,
cuckoo," or with my terrible singing voice, off key to say the
least, a very poor man's version of "Jamaica Farewell." Jay falls
asleep instantly. Every night this pattern repeats.

And then comes the trauma of divorce, problems everywhere, errant behavior, poor grades, multiple schools. And through each of his travails, my heart grew — until I knew compassion on a grand scale. Some fathers, when they look at their sons, see athletic achievements, scholastic awards, extracurricular accomplishments. But I see the sweetest, gentlest soul I know and my heart overflows with love and my compassion for his suffering knows no bounds.

10

My Children,
My Broken Heart

THERE IS ONE SUBJECT that everyone agrees on: your children cause you more pain than anything or anyone else in life, whether through their actions or their suffering. Few parents really understand what it's like to be a *divorced child,* moving back and forth between houses, always missing one parent, blaming yourself for the parents' divorce. After divorce, every one of the numerous partings is deeply hurtful, to the children and to the parent. I can't imagine what my children suffered.

"Where are my favorite toys, my stuffed rabbit, my blue blouse, my hockey skates, my tennis racket? As soon as I get adjusted to Mom's house, I have to move back to Daddy's."

No matter how you try, no vacation or celebration is as good as when the mother and father are both present. The beautiful idyllic world of the child is smashed — sometimes suddenly out of the blue or, other times, after terrible fighting between the parents.

I now live in the ultimate party house. The house has two floors. On the main entry level is the living room, dining room, kitchen and my bedroom. On the floor below are the children's and guest bedrooms, bar, media room, pool table, and stereo. The house is solidly built and noise doesn't travel far. Each room has its own private entrance. So teenage "guests" do not announce their arrival or departure by coming through the front door. This makes for an ideal location for a party. A deaf father upstairs, silent and undeterred access.

Sleep is a precious commodity, wherever you are. I rise early to work, and I'm asleep by 11:00 p.m. For teenagers the action doesn't begin until midnight. So, I'm often fast asleep before the party begins. How many parties were there? What horrors went on? How many times was I disappointed? I'm embarrassed and ashamed to tell you. How many times did I forgive? How many broken promises? No one will ever know except me and God. Would some errant teenager put a cement block in front of a blind person? But it's all right to take advantage of your deaf dad. What he doesn't know won't hurt him.

Teenage years are difficult for most parents, particularly divorced parents, and perhaps more difficult still for a deaf father who can't hear what's going on and really is "out of it" in many ways. Teenagers act out time-honored traditions, and children of divorce are venting their anger and hurt. I believed for a long time that my teenage children didn't love me, and loving them as much as I did, in combination with loneliness, deafness, guilt, and internal conflicts, took me down to the Grand Canyon of suffering.

11

The Unknown Life of
Late-Deafened Adults

---

*In [the Buddha's] view, the spiritual life cannot begin until
people allow themselves to be invaded by the reality of suffering, realize how fully it permeates our whole experience,
and feel the pain of all other beings, even those whom we
do not find congenial.* —Karen Armstrong, *Buddha*

IT'S THE EIGHTY-SECOND BIRTHDAY of the father of a close
friend and I'm hosting a small party for him. He was a fighter
pilot in World War II and is almost totally deaf. I watch him
at many social events. He never says anything because he obvi-
ously doesn't hear a word. If a face tells what a person is like,
then he is one of the sweetest men on the face of the earth. He
is almost angelic. As I engage him in conversation, making sure
he hears my questions, his face lights up with an indescribable
joy. If you've ever seen this happen to a reclusive, deaf person,
you will never forget it.

The world of late-deafened adults is poorly understood. As I
circulated early drafts of this book among my friends and relatives, I found to my amazement that virtually no one knew the
difficulty of my situation. My friends say, "You carry your deafness so well, no one knows you aren't hearing." There is a reason
for this. I have learned you can't stop the flow of group conversation. Also, you cannot control the environment. People's
dining rooms have bad acoustics or poor lighting. People take

you to dinner at noisy restaurants. Friends unconsciously turn away from you when they speak. Your host has a mustache, so you can't lip-read. A dozen things can "go wrong" — and there's *nothing* you can do about it.

Years ago, I attended several conferences for late-deafened adults. I found them sad and depressing, and I stopped going. Consider two conference topics: "What to Do When You Lose Your Job" and "How to Cope When Your Spouse Leaves You." Many of these people were withdrawing from the world, a huge, invisible tragedy.

Unless you are deaf, or have a deaf relative or spouse, you don't really know what our life is like. There are no good books describing the experience of late-deafened adults. I hope to raise consciousness about the travails of late-deafened adults and to help others understand how to communicate with us. I ask your compassion for the tens of millions of people like me who suffer silently, the extent of our pain unknown and perhaps unappreciated.

How do you raise consciousness? One way is to show examples of *sensitivity* and *insensitivity*. It is hard to do this without appearing to judge others. When women wrote about their need for liberation or gays and minorities about their shabby treatment in society, they were at first very strident. Despite the change in society's attitude, discrimination is still present. It takes a long time to alter behavior, and some people *can't* or *won't* change. I have tried to influence people's attitudes toward the deaf in casual conversation with little impact. Maybe this book will help.

Most books on deafness deal with people who are born deaf and live exclusively in the deaf world. Late-deafened adults don't want to live in the deaf world. They have no interest in "signing." They want to live in the hearing world. The number of severely hearing impaired adults is increasing rapidly. People are living longer. The noise, stresses, and side effects of modern life damage hearing. Loss can arrive with shocking swiftness. A good friend of mine recently reached the age of fifty. He went to an audiologist and, to his amazement, learned he had lost 40 percent of his hearing.

We are compassionate for handicapped people, those in wheelchairs, the blind, the ill, and the disabled. But it is my experience that few people offer the same compassion or have the same patience with deaf or hard-of-hearing people. Some people think of hearing loss as a nuisance and inconvenience for *themselves*. The Americans with Disabilities Act requires parking places near building entrances and sidewalk ramps, wheelchair access in buildings and bathrooms, and Braille on elevator buttons. Little is provided for the hearing impaired, beyond amplification for public telephones. There are no closed-captioned options in movie theaters. There's no assistance for the hearing impaired at athletic events. Waiters at restaurants communicate the "specials" only verbally.

Deafness means constant failure. Every communication — whether with the waiter at a restaurant, the clerk at a hotel, the airport check-in person, the customs official, your young children or grandchildren — involves failure and stress. You are unable to gauge the suitability and character of your young children's friends because you can't hear what they say. When your daughter stays out beyond her curfew, there's no one to call or speak to. When you are at the depths of loneliness, you can't pick up the phone and call someone. The reverse is also true. When friends are in need, you can't dial a number and offer them support. You must have enormous resiliency to fail at the most basic form of human interaction and retain your spirit.

In the early 1990s, I traveled frequently from White Plains to Philadelphia on a commuter airline. Commuter flights left every two or three minutes from a wide variety of gates. The planes took off within minutes of boarding. There was no electronic bulletin for flight information. Unable to hear the loudspeaker announcement, I was terrified I would miss my flight.

Deafness leads to isolation and loneliness. You retreat from life; you withdraw from social contact. You avoid parties, weddings, and restaurants — in fact, any social gathering.

A book written many years ago by a deaf woman makes an ironic observation. As the author approaches a group of her "friends," one of the women whispers to another, "Here comes Gail. Watch how she smiles at everything you say."

Increased deafness brings fear. In the mid-1980s, when my hearing loss accelerated, I never imagined I would be totally deaf in ten years. In the spring of 1988, I went skiing in New Mexico. Maybe the high altitude reduced circulation to my auditory nerve. Who knows? Six weeks later, my "good ear" was totally deaf. The suddenness of the loss scared me profoundly. I knew then it was only a matter of time until my other ear left me for the next world. But that knowledge did nothing to eliminate my growing fear of the unknown and the mounting stress I felt as I tried to cope in a world that was becoming quieter and quieter.

In 1993, I moved to Sun Valley, Idaho. It seemed like a warm and secure place. It's a small town with friendly people, so I hoped I could live with less fear and stress. Yet at times I thought my life was over. There were scores of nights that I felt so depressed and lonely that I didn't want to keep on living if tomorrow was as bad as today. But tomorrow is always a better day.

A friend reads the first draft of this book and says, "What should I do so you can hear me better?" A good question, and here's my answer: Speak clearly. Enunciate carefully. Speak slowly. Project your voice. Never talk to me when my back is turned, your back is turned, or if you are not close to me. Face me when you talk. Do not mumble. Do not put your hands in front of your face. Clarity is more important than loudness.

Watch my eyes and my face to see if I understand. If I don't register recognition, use different words to say the same thing.

Suppose you say, "How was your tennis match yesterday?" "Tennis" and "match" are both hard words to lip-read, so I don't understand you. You could try some alternatives, such as

"How was your game yesterday?" or "Did you win?" or "How did you play yesterday?"

You tell me, "Harry was hurt!" I can't understand you.

Perhaps say, "Rhonda's husband, Harry, was in a car accident." You say, "I'm in a hurry!" I may not understand you.

A possible alternative: "I'm in a rush!" or "I can't be late!"

When I speak to foreigners in English, I try to use simple vocabulary. If I don't see recognition on their face, I express the same thought three or four different ways until I see a light of understanding.

This is not hard to do.

Repeating the same words over and over again often does not help deaf people understand. If you change the wording, particularly the key words, you have a better chance of getting your point across.

If you want me to understand you, I can't do it alone.

12

I Confess My Fears

One of the sure paths to the real future (because there is
also a false future) is to proceed in the direction of your
fear. — Milorad Pavic, Dictionary of the Khazars

MAYBE THERE ARE SOME courageous people who never have
a moment of fear. I'm not one of them. My theory is that
if you aren't afraid, you haven't had a trauma. Impending deafness frightened me greatly. I had a fear of the unknown, I worried
whether my friends would see the burden of a friendship with a
deaf person as too much effort, and whether a woman would be
interested in me. I feared that my children might be embarrassed
to have me meet their friends. I was afraid of being humiliated
when people asked me questions I couldn't hear. Deafness frequently results in a career change. Few people are in a business
where they don't need hearing. This can be especially traumatic,
already adding to all the other stresses. Will I be able to support
myself?

I am in Boston one cold, rainy winter morning. I'm at a large
table. There are twenty-five or more people. Most of them, as
usual, sit at the far end. I am frighteningly alone. I'm aware that
many people take minutes to ask a question, so asking them to
repeat any question is impractical. I'm there to give an important
presentation, and I am so fearful of being asked a question, not
hearing it, and appearing "deaf and dumb" that my hands trem-
ble and my head is so nervous that I have to hold it in my hand
to keep from shaking. This has happened to me many times. I

fear and hate these sessions with all my being. Yet this is part of keeping my word to myself: don't retreat; don't avoid something because you are deaf. Force yourself to confront your fears and deal with them as best you can.

On this occasion, someone at the far side of the room asked questions that I couldn't hear. When he started speaking, I knew it would be a disaster, the king of mumblers, rambling for minutes, so I had no idea what the topic was. So I did what I could with a bad hand: I answered every conceivable question I thought he could have asked and tried to make my answers as interesting as possible so no one would mind if I didn't answer correctly.

I remember going through Mexican customs in the early 1990s. Heavy accents in any language make lipreading almost impossible. Perhaps I still have my father's legacy of nervousness at immigration. The Mexican official asked me a question I couldn't understand. He was not polite, and there were people behind me anxious to proceed in line. No matter how many times he repeated the question, I couldn't understand what he wanted. What was going to happen to me? How could I ever extricate myself from this horror? After guessing incorrectly many times, I finally figured out what he was asking. How many repetitions, I asked, would I have of this humiliating incident? If you are traveling with another person, your companion can help you with the question, but in this case, as many other times, I was alone.

In 1992, I organized a train trip for a few friends across China. We joined a larger group that was sponsored by the American Museum of Natural History. There were seven of my friends and about seventy in the group overall. The trip retraced the old Silk Route, and we were traveling on a private train consisting of eight Soviet-built "luxury" cars from the 1930s. I successfully persuaded my friends to join the group by repeating the claim in the marketing brochure that there would be a dining car for each type of Chinese cuisine. The reality was something entirely different. Not only did I never dare look at how the food was prepared, but suffice it to say that breakfast, lunch, and dinner for the entire two-week trip, was the same meal.

The trip began in Beijing and ended in Urumchi, equivalent to taking a train from Washington, D.C., to Seattle. I was very careful with the water as I am in all developing countries. Nevertheless, while I was shaving, some of the water from the "luxury" bathrooms must have gotten into my ear and caused a major infection. Only a few days into the trip, at Xian, the infection became very uncomfortable. I was faced with a dilemma: leave the trip, abandon my guests and friends, and seek a doctor's help, or stay on the trip with the prospect of no medical assistance for nearly two weeks. There would be no phones, faxes, or contact with the outside world. I couldn't abandon my friends, I concluded, and so I went on. The infection worsened and became more painful. Did I tell you that the infection was in my only hearing ear? Did I tell you that ear infections can ruin hearing and that I was fearful that I might lose what little hearing I had left?

A few days later, in the middle of the night, I awoke with excruciating pain in my ear. It was almost unbearable. I was terribly frightened. What was happening? Was I losing the rest of my hearing? Was I stupid to put loyalty to friends before my hearing? Had I made an incredibly stupid choice? I couldn't deal with this by myself. I knocked on the compartment door of one of my friends. "Will you help me? I don't know what's happening. I'm terrified. I'm going deaf. The pain is unbearable." She held me most of the night until the pain subsided. As it turns out, without my knowledge, the train had gone over an enormous mountain range, and the altitude plus the infection was causing the pain.

The two American doctors traveling as part of the group refused to help me because they didn't want to accept responsibility if something went wrong. However, a psychiatrist from New Orleans eventually gave me drops for the infection, which "miraculously" cleared up as the train pulled into Urumchi. There was no damage done to my hearing, as far as I could see, but the damage to my psyche was unforgettable.

13

Deaf Like Me

GOING DEAF, in my case, was a long process. I have friends who lost their hearing overnight. I was lucky. I had years to prepare — emotionally, professionally, and tactically. My first memory of something amiss was at age fourteen. I could not hear the words of songs, as all my friends could, and I was very perplexed. The next signal occurred in college. Loud music, noisy bars, rock bands — we never congregated in a quiet place, and hearing became increasingly difficult. My friends complained that I said "what?" over and over. They teased me so unmercifully that I visited an audiologist during Christmas vacation. I discovered I had a significant loss in the high-frequency-speech range. It was the first of hundreds of hearing tests. I came to hate them. I already knew I was losing my hearing, so why go through this grueling process, with no apparent benefit?

What was the cause of deafness? Could it be stopped? Reversed? For some reason, my parents were in denial, or so it seemed to me. I kept hoping that as a doctor and research scientist, my father would take a leadership role in my case. But perhaps he already knew the answer and accepted it with a quiet fatality. The acceleration of my hearing loss in my sophomore and junior years was acute. I began looking for a possible cause. I suffered from severe allergies, and I wondered whether the hearing loss was allergy-related. Every morning I woke up sneezing, sometimes for hours on end. My sinuses and nostrils were totally blocked. I had a sinus infection almost from the time I was twelve until decades later, when a smart ear, nose, and throat doctor gave me cortisone shots. If your sinus cavity is swollen, then maybe the hearing mechanism is also swollen. Maybe, the ears are not getting enough blood, and nerves are dying.

This hypothesis was validated by a famous Boston doctor whom I met one weekend at Cape Cod. He told me there was considerable scientific evidence that allergies cause hearing loss. I am allergic to dust, ragweed, trees, pets, and many foods and liquids. As one allergy doctor said, "You're allergic to the ubiquitous things." I began a long series of allergy tests and injections for years and years, with different doctors in different places. But nothing seemed to help.

I moved to New York City and began working. I found I had severe difficulty participating in business lunches at restaurants. I also found I was making errors in taking down phone numbers. The years of my twenties were incredibly stressful. I spent my day on the telephone as a researcher and investigative reporter, struggling to understand what people said. I developed a technique. I repeated what the person said — accuracy was important — because this was for publication. After eight hours a day of this Herculean effort to gather accurate information, I was so exhausted I did not want to see or talk to anyone. Imagine you are on a cell phone and the person on the other end fades in and out. That's the way it feels. Except you can't say, "This is a poor connection; can I call you back?" You have to make do.

My ears gradually clogged and never seemed to unclog. It was a more powerful and uncomfortable version of the blocked ears that come when you already have a severe cold and then you experience a sudden descent in the elevator of a high-rise building or in an airplane. I visited doctors and implored them to find a way to clear the blockage. They tried everything from injections into my sinuses to blowing out my ear. The blockage grew more severe, and one doctor told me it would never improve. "It's a permanent symptom of hearing loss," he said.

I tried every type of phone amplifier. Some of them worked for a while, but not for long. I graduated to stronger and stronger amplifiers, eventually settling on the Walker Clarity phone because loudness does not necessarily give better comprehension. I started with standard hearing aids, graduated to Bosch, which specialized in high-frequency loss at the time, to the world's most powerful hearing aid.

Nevertheless, as a precaution, I began lipreading classes. I found a soul mate for a teacher. Her name is Fran Santore, and she helped me with the emotional impact of hearing loss. After years of hard study, she transformed me into a first-rate lip-reader, an invaluable talent as my hearing eroded. As my hearing loss worsened, there came a day when I was unable to understand anyone on the phone, not even my mother, children, or friends.

Then another day came. I was unable to comprehend one-on-one conversations. My friends had to write down for me what they said. I could never find the words to tell you how sad this was.

But I was lucky in one sense. I began a correspondence with an exceptional woman in Boston. Her name was Joanne. She was very intelligent and complex. I talked on the phone and she faxed me back her response. It was actually a wonderful way to communicate. No interruptions!

I sometimes spoke for thirty minutes at a time. She then responded with a ten- or fifteen-page fax and later often a ten-page letter. In two years, I filled a four-foot by two-foot by two-foot box containing her letters and faxes. The subjects we talked about were very intimate. Extremely personal. People sometimes think faxes are public property, and my household felt free to read them. So I moved the fax machine into my bedroom closet, which helped but didn't solve the problem.

I still had to talk on the phone for business. At first, we would put the caller on a speakerphone, and my associates took notes. Then, my assistant had the brilliant idea that typing was faster than writing. So we put a computer in the conference room, and whenever anyone called, she typed the conversation on the computer screen. This was a vast improvement. Unfortunately, I was unable to hear the nuances in people's voices. I didn't know whether they were happy or angry or impatient or cold. I didn't know when they finished talking. I frequently interrupted unintentionally. Since my assistant was a slow typist, I missed a lot, sometimes an entire conversation. There was a long lag time between a question and its appearance on the computer screen. But this was better than not using the phone at all.

Meanwhile, the deterioration in my hearing continued relentlessly. Then one morning I woke up and could no longer hear my own voice.

14

How I Confront a Dilemma

‎--------‎
‎------‎
‎----‎

A SSERT YOURSELF! Raise consciousness! Turn the music off!
Turn up the lights! No, I won't go to that restaurant, it's
too noisy. Will you stop laughing so loudly! I can't hear when
everyone talks at once! Don't turn your face away! The greatest
quandary facing a deaf person is how assertive you should be.
Because late-deafened people are reclusive and lonely, they drift
deeper and deeper into their own world. Spouses or children
drag them to social events. But they have been pushed down so
hard for so long, they don't remember how to push back or ask
or assert, if they ever knew.

I'm at a friend's house in Colorado for an annual ski weekend.
There are about twenty of us at a square table. I talk briefly about
my hearing loss and the effect it has had on my life. Afterward,
one of the participants, a lecturer in history, comes up to me
and explains that he has a deaf student in one of his classes
and tells me he now plans to be much more sensitive to this
hardship. The professor has a large beard and mustache and his
lips are entirely hidden, a lip-reader's nightmare. I explain how
hard it is to lip-read a man with heavy facial hair. Later his
wife, also a professor of history, is giving a lecture. She shows
us a slide presentation of ancient art. The overhead light is on
at the beginning of her presentation, but after a few minutes,
her husband turns the lights off. Without lights, I can no longer
comprehend her lecture, but the twenty people in the room see
the intricate beauty of the slides more clearly.

The dilemma? Do nothing, miss the lecture, enjoy the slide show, and be happy that everyone has a clear view of this beautiful, ancient art? Or make a fuss and turn the lights back on? Of course, I choose to remain silent, as I have a thousand times, when people turn down the lights, turn up the music, take me to noisy restaurants, and talk at the same time, interrupting each other constantly.

I'm at a dinner party with five other people. I'm sitting in the middle of the table with a woman on my right, a woman on my left, and three people across from me. I'm already totally deaf in my left ear, so I have to turn my head all the way to the left, exposing my right ear to the center, to have any chance of hearing. The woman on my right, "hearing" ear is very boisterous and noisy. She laughs loudly almost all evening. She is in a hilarious dialogue with a woman across the table. They are having a very good time, but are so noisy that I can't hear the conversation I'm trying to conduct with the man across from me.

Here's my dilemma. Do I ask these two women to please quiet down, which would put a damper on their enthusiasm? Or do I join in the fun and laughter and have a good time? It's a dilemma and choice we late-deafened adults face. Of course, I choose the latter, as I always have. I can't speak for others. This is how I resolve it, and I never have any regrets.

15

The Late, Lamented Dr. Gould

W E'VE ALL HEARD stories of callous and incompetent doctors. Here's a story of a great doctor, a man of enormous
compassion. He treated me like his only patient. His name was
Dr. Jim Gould. He had an office in New York City in the
East Seventies between Madison and Park. I came to know him
through my good friend Ed Ney, who had trouble with his vocal
chords. Ed said, "If anyone can help you, it's Dr. Gould."

I had visited many doctors with no results. Dr. Gould was a
famous ear, nose, and throat specialist. He had helped dozens
of the world's most famous singers. His office was filled with
affectionately autographed pictures from all the best-known vo-
calists. As soon as I met Dr. Gould, I knew I was in the care of
a great specialist. I was confident, no matter what the outcome,
that he would handle my case and explore every possible avenue.
That's all you can ever expect or hope for. Did I try every rem-
edy, visit every specialist? If you have seen the best, and he tries
everything, then you can accept your loss. But what if you give
up early, and there is a therapy that might work? On the other
hand, you don't want to search endlessly for a cure if deafness
is inevitable and irreversible.

Dr. Gould sent me to one of the country's most advanced and
creative specialists, Dr. Wallace Rubin in Metairie, Louisiana.
My first visit in the late 1980s took me through three days of
tests, from 5:00 a.m. until 10:00 p.m. That may sound grueling,
but I *wanted* to be tested. I was tired of ear doctors who looked

at my hearing chart and said, "There's nothing we can do." I wanted an expert to give me every test known to man.

Dr. Rubin is a leading expert on allergies. He put me on a special diet: unlimited meat, chicken, and fish, no dairy, no sugar, and only a hundred grams of carbohydrates a day. Within two weeks, I lost twenty pounds. I devoured protein ravenously, sometimes finishing the main course before other people started. Sugar is in everything. If you check the labels, you'll see there is sugar in ketchup, milk, cold cereal, bread, crackers — you name it, sugar is everywhere. I continued with the diet for two years. The diet may have slowed the hearing loss, but did not stop it. I visited Dr. Rubin four times a year. Dr. Gould checked on my progress, monitoring all the data. Dr. Gould introduced me to other world-class experts: Dr. Bob Ruben of Albert Einstein College of Medicine and Dr. Chuck Berlin of LSU Medical.

Chuck Berlin was doing advanced research on hair cell rejuvenation. Hair cells are microscopic amplifiers for the human ear, an essential element of hearing. Most deafness is caused when hair cells die. People with normal hearing have thirty thousand hair cells in each ear. Dr. Berlin tested me and found that I had five hundred. Clearly, there was some defect in my genetic makeup that caused my hair cells to self-destruct. Berlin noted that hair cells can be restored in other mammals. He was researching a way to rejuvenate hair cells in humans. He thought the cure was close. So did Dr. Gould, who believed hair cell restoration could help me soon. Both of them were premature. But it didn't matter. They gave me hope at a time when there was little hope.

Albert Einstein Hospital is located in the Bronx. It can take an hour or more to get there from midtown Manhattan. Every time I visited Dr. Ruben, Dr. Gould also made the trip, despite a backlog of patients that a dozen doctors could barely handle. Due to Dr. Gould's efforts, I had four out of the top five ear doctors in the United States focusing on my hearing loss. Dr. Gould showed me a note that he carried in his wallet with my telephone number as a reminder: "Is there a new cure for Kiril?"

In the fall of 1987 I was hospitalized with intense back pain. I was on Demerol for a week and, to my surprise, I noticed a major improvement in hearing. I mentioned this to Dr. Gould, who believed patients know their own bodies and doctors should listen to them. So with Dr. Ruben's approval we experimented with Demerol injections, combined with hearing tests. The experiment was not successful. But it showed the open mindedness of the compassionate Dr. Gould.

Another ear doctor behaved in stark contrast with Dr. Gould. Reluctantly, I agreed to see a specialist whom a friend recommended. Without any fanfare, the doctor asked to see my hearing charts. After briefly scanning them, he said, "You will be totally deaf in five years." Of course he was right, but brutal!

One day, Dr. Gould asked me to visit his office. He introduced me to Jerry Fox, who raises money for research on hair cell rejuvenation. I assisted Jerry Fox for years, and she does incredible work. If and when hair cells are rejuvenated, I am sure she will have played a major part.

Despite the efforts of these devoted doctors, I went deaf. Yet I will never forget their kindness and caring. I owe them a huge debt of gratitude. When Dr. Gould passed away in 1994, two thousand people attended his funeral. Some of the world's greatest opera singers sang in his honor — a fitting ending to a great man's career.

16

The Ringing in My Ears

RINGING IN THE EARS is particularly frightening. You can be aware of your hearing loss, even resigned to it, but the ringing is a message, a never-ending, relentless message. I found that my ears rang more when I was under stress, on airplanes, and at high altitudes. As mentioned, I lost the hearing in my left ear six weeks after spending a vacation in high-altitude Santa Fe. I was so worried about the impact of altitude that I consulted with Dr. Gould, who looked for research papers connecting altitude with hearing loss. At high altitudes, perhaps the blood flow to the ear is weakened, further accelerating the nerve loss. Dr. Gould put me on a complicated medication with potential side effects, so the treatment had to be carefully monitored.

There are various types of ringing — a soft buzzing, a violent and loud ringing like thunder, and occasionally a ringing like a tornado coming through an echo chamber. When I suddenly lost the hearing in my left ear, it was the echo-chamber version that signaled the change. It was one of the most terrifying sounds in the world, I assure you. Until I went deaf, I had constant ringing in my ears. It might lessen for a week, even a month — but it never stopped. And with that ringing came the reminder that I was going deaf. Of course, I already knew this, but did I need to be reminded every second of every day? Kiril, the deafness bell rings for *you*. You can't run, and you can't hide.

17

Smiling on the Outside, Crying on the Inside

WHEN I'M WITH a group of people, I try to smile. It's not always easy, but I think it's a very important act for a deaf person. When someone greets me with enthusiasm and a big smile, I never forget. You connect to that person, and that smile reaches you deeply.

A deaf person does *not* hear group conversation. What do you do about it? How do you behave? My approach is to smile. I want everyone to think I'm hearing, participating and having a great time. Suppose I do the opposite — sit morosely in the corner, feeling sorry for myself. My bad mood might sour the atmosphere. I deliberately *pretend* to hear. But I still enjoy the evening because I don't allow myself to feel isolated.

I exchange looks with people, laugh at the jokes I don't hear, smile when someone is telling me a story I don't fully comprehend. Of course, a little part of me is crying on the inside. But the more I smile, the less I cry. My choice. And if someone says about me, "watch how he smiles at everything you say," then so be it.

18

The Loss You Can't Control

IN THE SPRING of 2001 I visited a psychic. I told him nothing about my life or past. I simply listened. The psychic told me things about myself, and others close to me, which he could never have known without special insight. I began to think there is more predeterminism than I had believed: fate, destiny, the will of God, your stars, call it what you will.

Consider this scene from *Lawrence of Arabia*. Lawrence and Prince Feisal are crossing the desert to invade Aqaba from the unprotected, desert side. A man falls off his camel, but is not immediately missed. Lawrence returns to the worst part of the desert to rescue him. Prince Feisal warns Lawrence not to go. "It is written," he says.

At great personal risk and sacrifice, Lawrence finds the man and brings him back. Lawrence is now a hero. A day later, two of the tribes, always uneasy with each other, erupt. A man is killed. But who should punish the murderer? Lawrence is chosen to kill the man. He agrees — to preserve the peace and his cherished dream of uniting Arabia. As the man turns his face, Lawrence sees it is the one whom he had saved. Lawrence pulls the trigger, and Feisal says, "You see, it *was* written."

In my case, deafness *was* written. I fought the advance of deafness with every ounce of my being. I fought and fought and fought and fought. And fought and fought and fought. I would adjust to each new level of hearing, and ask God for a short respite, a month or two, a few weeks. I had adjusted. I could deal with this level. But, no, the loss continued. Deafness waits for no man.

Beethoven produced many of his greatest works when he was deaf. Many music lovers, myself included, believe he was the greatest composer of all time. Imagine Beethoven's piano, no legs, resting directly on the floor. Think of the composer of the Ninth Symphony, stone deaf, with an ear pressed to the floor, desperate to catch a vibration. On his deathbed, Beethoven sat up and shook his fist at the heavens. No one knows why, but I can suggest a good reason: frustration and anger at deafness.

In certain aspects, deafness changed my philosophy. For most of my life, I believed that if you worked hard enough, you'd succeed. If you wanted something enough, you could get it. As Churchill said, "Never give in! Never give in! Never, never, never. Never — in anything great or small, large or petty — never give in except to convictions of honor and good sense."

Of course, there may be disappointments and setbacks. But somewhere on the road to deafness, I realized another truth; there is a force greater than you. You stand on the beach, feet planted firmly in the sand, jaw set and determined, muscles tensed — and suddenly a tidal wave comes and flattens you. I came to accept that deafness was bigger than I was. I lay down before this superior force, God's will, my destiny, and swam with the current. This revelation was perhaps the most profound, emotional experience in my life, more so than going deaf or getting divorced.

When I was sixteen, I spent a good portion of a summer mourning the end of a relationship with a girl. I don't even remember who she is or what happened. But I do remember what my father said. "Kiril, put your problems in the proper context. Perhaps the universe is infinite. Suppose it continues to expand at this same incredible pace, forever. By comparison, your problem is so tiny!" I can say that deafness made me strong. I lost and lost and lost again. I faced and overcame fear and stress and loneliness and isolation. I also learned that certain things are written. Only a fool fights destiny.

19

Frustration Pushes Me
to the Edge

IN THE EARLY 1990s I discovered the investment opportunities in Hong Kong. The stock market was selling at about seven times earnings, with a 4.5 percent dividend yield and the best earnings record in the world over the past thirty years. Hong Kong was selling at a "China discount." I believed it should sell at a "China premium." I organized many trips to Hong Kong and China for my clients to show them the opportunities. China was awakening economically, and it was a historic opportunity. Each trip involved a week or ten days of company meetings in Hong Kong and travels to Guangdong Province in China to meet top government officials. The day began at 7:00 a.m. and ended at midnight.

As discussed, heavy Chinese accents are virtually impossible for me to comprehend. So I spent these days understanding nothing that was said. I was the host and was unable to ask a question because it might already have been asked and answered. Of all the participants, who do you think was the most interested in hearing the discussions? Of all the participants, who do you think was most upset at missing what was said?

I have a passionate, intellectual curiosity about many things. I frequently meet people who are very knowledgeable in their fields. I am excited beyond words to learn from them and to understand more about their expertise. Over the years, I have encountered literally hundreds of such people. I ask questions —

desperate to know the answers — and am unable to hear. During these episodes, the frustration inside me reaches such an intensity that I feel like screaming. Other times, I'm so depressed I fall into the blackest and bleakest mood.

At first you want what you can't have, then the frustration reaches the point of maximum intensity, and afterward it can only subside. The peak of frustration brought me to the "source," and then I accepted it and began to acquire inner peace. Now I say, "What *can* you do?" And isn't that the ultimate truth about so many of life's travails and tragedies?

20

My Friend Joan

You cannot teach a man anything; you can only help him find it within himself.　　　　　　　　　　　　　— Galileo

I'VE KNOWN JOAN for thirty years. We remain close and corre- spond frequently even though we live in different cities and, sometimes, on different continents. Joan professes she loves me deeply, yet sometimes I wonder. There is no one with whom I have a greater difficulty communicating. Joan is what you might call neurotic. Her mouth is tense. She frequently giggles ner- vously. She speaks fast, in a high voice, doesn't move her lips, laughs *and* giggles. I rarely understand anything she says. When I started lip-reading classes, I implored Joan to visit my teacher to learn how to speak to me so I could understand. She never went.

One night we went out to dinner with friends in Greenwich Village. On the way back in the taxi, I said, "Do you realize that I didn't understand one word you said all night. I didn't hear any of your jokes or anything else. Nothing. Nada. Do you get it?" I looked at her intensely. "Maybe you don't care whether I hear or not. Maybe you were talking only to Bill and Sally. But if you want me to participate, you will have to change the way you speak." Of course, nothing changed.

A year later, I spent an evening with Joan. I resolved to change tactics. We were sitting in a Japanese restaurant on Second Av- enue. Joan spoke, enunciating in the same way she always had, incomprehensible to me. I didn't understand a word of it.

"I didn't hear you," I said.

She repeated it.

"I don't understand what you said."

She spoke again.

"I didn't understand you."

She repeated again.

"I didn't understand what you said."

And so on.

There are other people like Joan. If you ask them, they will tell you they adore animals and consider themselves very compassionate and loving people. But are they? When you are with a handicapped person, you have to change. We do it for the blind and people with other disabilities. Why not the deaf?

21

I Don't Hear,
but I Listen

DICK BARKER is one of the most prominent men in his field. He is analytical and observant. We are having lunch in Hailey, Idaho, at an outdoor restaurant formerly owned by Bruce Willis. Barker turns to me and says, "You are the best listener I've ever met. It's probably because hearing is so precious to you." This is a great compliment.

Dale Carnegie tells the following story: He is sitting next to a woman at a dinner party. He listens to her with close attention and never says a word. The next day, the hostess calls him. The dinner companion has raved about Carnegie's great conversational skills.

I have spent thousands of hours watching people talk, usually not hearing them. You could say I'm a professional bystander. What I see is this: there are few people *really* listening. Many people interrupt, not only when others are talking, but even the answers to their own questions. I also wonder whether certain people can't understand each other no matter what they do. Their personalities are so different that they literally speak a different language. Sasha Migunov, the Russian writer from Florida, believes that some people are simply unable to understand each other due to different life experiences, philosophies of life, and mental rigidity. It's certainly a possibility, although I find the thought depressing.

Hearing is precious to me, so I value listening as one of the great pastimes of life. Listening is a lost art. Take the typical married couple. If you are out on a foursome, time and again, I see the following: as soon as one spouse or partner begins to talk, the other one starts another conversation. Neither one wants to listen to the other; maybe the stories and conversations have been told too many times. Many couples socialize non-stop — perhaps so they never have to sit down with one another, look each other in the eye, and *talk*. I believe communication is really *semantics*. I am very careful about the words I use. I am a writer and know the meaning of words.

One evening I was sitting outside on my terrace looking at the mountains. I was having dinner with Allyn Stewart. She is extremely smart, a very successful movie producer, and someone with excellent taste, so I always listen very closely to everything she says. Allyn has it all — a compassionate heart, an enlightened spirit, passion, determination, courage, and excellent judgment.

I say, "Despite what some people think, I really want to get married again." This has long been a topic of conversation among my friends.

"If you say it, I believe you."

I am overcome by this simple reaction — say it, and I'll believe you! So many people are caught up in their own perception of you that even if they hear you they don't or won't listen. This is an example of listening where the full benefit of communication is realized. If people don't listen to each other, how can they successfully communicate?

Frequently, someone will say, "This is what you told me."

"That's not what I said. I don't use those words. That wasn't my meaning."

People often hear what they want to hear based on their own emotional baggage and their experiences with the other person. Put another way, we see life through a prism that validates our own impressions and biases. Is this communication?

I have a friend from Miami whose name is Steve Herbits. He's a certified, walking genius. When Steve and I talk, I invariably reach for a pen and paper and take notes. Steve never tries to impress me, never puts his ego in the conversation. There is no grandstanding. We debate and interact on many ideas and subjects. In general, as soon as any conversation becomes personal, defenses set in and the quality of the conversation immediately deteriorates. Dick Barker is right in one sense. Understanding what a person says is uncommonly precious to me. Maybe the *most* precious of life's gifts, as we shall see.

22

Openness Leads to Growth

M ANY LATE-DEAFENED ADULTS have someone who takes care of them — a spouse, daughter, son, sister, brother, or friend. This person is responsible for bringing the world to their door.

A friend of mine wrote a biography of the wife of a famous artist. The wife kept a comprehensive daily diary. Their social life reads like a *Who's Who* of the artistic and literary world: James Joyce, Pablo Picasso, William Butler Yeats, and Virginia Woolf, to name a few. Her diary tells nothing of the conversations that transpired, only discussing what she wore that night, the food served at dinner, and other superficialities. Imagine this woman was your lifeline to the world, later summarizing the evening by telling you about the six courses at a restaurant, the dress style of the women, and her own mood that night — when Picasso had talked about art. I sometimes feel this same frustration when I ask people to evaluate the character of our dinner companions, what happened, what did they talk about, what did *you* learn tonight? When you are deaf, you are totally dependent on your companion and his or her insight, memory, curiosity, intelligence, and profundity.

Consider the case of Suzy Stewart, a companion of mine for several years. Before she was laid off during downsizing, Suzy was a vice president at Bloomingdale's. She was one of the first retailers to start the trend of outsourcing to developing countries. She tells stories of negotiating with a dozen men in a sweat-shop in rural Turkey or China. Suzy is a strong and competent lady. She also has a good business mind. Suzy had a tough child-hood. Her father had multiple sclerosis, and she had to go to work to support the family at the age of sixteen. Later, her older brother committed suicide in a most gruesome way. I found out that while she was between jobs during the retailing crisis of the early 1990s she paid her mortgage with credit cards. She never complained, talked of her straitened finances, or asked for help.

Her intimate involvement with her father's failing health and other tragedies made Suzy extremely sensitive to my deafness and need to communicate. She made a herculean effort to com-municate with me, repeating what others said if she thought I didn't hear, exaggerating her lip movements, enunciating and projecting her voice. I would give her a perfect 10. I met Suzy at the worst part of my deafness, when I was totally dependent on others to feed me information on what was happening. She ac-companied me on several of my many trips to China and Hong Kong. After a dinner with Chinese or Hong Kong business as-sociates, I asked her for a recap of what was important. What did Victor mean when he asked me that question during dessert? How did Mr. Lien answer my question about infrastructure in China? What was that ten-minute conversation about at the end of the evening? Politics? Democracy in Hong Kong? Do you think these men are trustworthy? What do you think their agenda was? When the two Chinese talked excitedly with each other, what were they saying? What did Mr. Lien's wife say about her experience in the Cultural Revolution? Afterward I would often spend an hour or two asking Suzy questions. Even with her considerable observational skills and powers of retention, Suzy was often unable to satisfy my craving for information.

This leads to the greater question of how people learn and grow. Most people are the product of their experience, which means they have biases and prejudices that are hard to change. For years I have said that you can predict a person's behavior by finding out what was the last traumatic experience in that person's life. Time and time again, I have seen leaders of all kinds, businessmen, and investors ruined by their biases. Biases occur because people's minds are closed and their sources of information are, knowingly or unknowingly, restricted.

Up until the World Trade Center tragedy, most Americans were not interested in foreign news. Ninety-five percent of the world's population *doesn't* live in the United States. How can you not be vitally concerned with foreign news, cultures, trends, and policy issues? When you visit India, the newspapers give a different perspective on terrorism. For the past two decades, terrorism has been a way of life in India, and over seventy thousand people have been killed in such attacks.

Every day, I try to come to the major issues with an open mind and a willingness to reverse my position. This is not easy, and it requires discipline and openness. You suffer a lot of anguish when you are forced to change. That's why many people are reluctant to do it. The difficulty comes in maintaining a balance between deep beliefs and flexibility. If you go too far in either direction, you fall into trouble. Swinging around like a leaf in the wind is almost as bad as blind dogmatism.

I like change, particularly the challenge in seeing it early. I'm not threatened by change or reluctant to embrace it, as many others are. Deafness has made me more open to new information. Because my information flow via voice is restricted, deafness has made me see the enormous value of a wide-open mind. Openness is a crucial advantage in life's struggles. The more open I have become, the less handicapped I have felt — to the point that the growth of openness has nearly offset the loss of the ability to hear.

23

My Lifeline to the World
Goes Sour

I AM SITTING in an oversized armchair in my office in York-town, New York. It's the fall of 1990 and the trees are turning yellow. You can see the Catskill Mountains in the distance. I work in an all-glass building that sits high on a hill overlooking a reservoir. I'm interviewing a woman named Fiona for the position of personal assistant. She's tall with brown hair falling to her shoulders and big blue eyes. She recently moved to New York from Arizona because her aging mother is ill and can no longer care for herself.

I am recently divorced and share the parenting of my two young children. Fiona correctly sees my circumstances: a man who has lost his hearing, his family, and, as usually happens after divorce, his friends and social life. Fiona says, "Kiril, I would like to assist you any way I can. I'm sure you need help at home, and I want you to know that I'll do anything I can to make your life easier." She seems to be the right person at the right time.

Always a very independent man, I am now totally helpless. I can't make a phone call by myself. I'm unable to talk to my children's teachers about schoolwork. I can't talk to the doctor who calls with personal medical information. When the surgeon phones to talk about an emergency appendectomy he is performing on my daughter, I can't speak directly to him. Over the next four years, Fiona becomes as involved with my life as a person can be in a professional way. Since *all* communication with the outside world goes through Fiona, she knows every intimate detail about every aspect of my life. When a deaf person is intimate with someone, a special bond of trust forms. I am helpless, and I trust the person blindly. I am totally dependent on her or him for information — my precious lifeline to the world.

Three years after Fiona joins our company, she becomes engaged. She cries every day the week before her marriage. I ask her to lunch. What is the problem? She tells me her fiancé is immature and treats her badly. She fears she is making a big mistake. I tell her she should postpone the marriage.

She says, "What will I tell him? How can I disappoint my parents?"

"Better to end it now than have a bad marriage, which will inevitably lead to a more painful break down the road," I answer.

Fiona goes ahead with the marriage, and she is unhappy from the start.

A year later, she sends me a fax announcing that she needs to take time off due to marital stress. She disappears for two months. No one knows where she is. During this time, I hire an accountant to handle my personal finances. In reviewing my records, she finds a $3,500 personal check paid to a Visa account that is not mine. We soon discover that it is Fiona's account. When Fiona surfaces two months later, I ask my associate in Yorktown to diplomatically ask her for an explanation. According to his report, she becomes hostile. I am deeply hurt. I hope it is a clerical error.

I ponder for several weeks how I should handle it. I conclude this: how *she* behaves is not the issue; what is important is how *I* behave. I write her the following letter:

"Dear Fiona, This is a devastating and tragic moment. I'm sure you realize you can't work here again. I know your circumstances are difficult and that you would like to leave John and go off on your own. Accordingly, I'm going to send you a check for $10,000 to help you in this transition. All the best, Kiril."

I never receive a response. I learn later that Fiona — my life-line to the world — kept information from me and provided disinformation. Fiona had a life and death control over what information reached me. I had no way to verify what she told me. When you depend on someone to hear and communicate, you must rely on the integrity and judgment of that person. For late-deafened adults, the person who is your connection to the world can make or break you, depending on their trustworthiness, impartiality, and consideration.

Six years later, I get the following e-mail from Fiona:

"Kiril, I finally left John. I have had a tough time, but I'm hopeful for the future. I'm trying to put my life together. I want to enter the job force again, and I'm looking for work. Would you write me a letter of recommendation? Here's what I'd like you to say . . . "

I don't read any further. I respond as follows:

"Dear Fiona, I would like to help you, but I never received a thank you for the $10,000 I gave you. I never heard an explanation for the $3,500 that was paid to your Visa account."

Her response comes immediately:

"Kiril, forget the job recommendation. All I want is your forgiveness."

I respond equally fast:

"I forgive you."

She answers: "Kiril, you saved my life. You have given me hope again. I can't begin to tell you how much this means to me. God bless you, Kiril."

Most of us think injustice goes unpunished. I always did. I've read history, after all. But here's a story of how guilt festered in a woman — to the point that she craved absolution. Maybe there is more good in all of us than we realize.

24

Triumph over Adversity

A fool thinks himself to be wise, but a wise man knows himself to be a fool.
— William Shakespeare

SINCE 1983, I've been a consultant to CEOs, money managers, and financial institutions. I look for investment opportunities, secular trends, and their reversals. I attempt to anticipate change and try to explain the big picture. I couldn't have a better career. It allows me to read, think, and write. It's a good fit with deafness, and deafness made me better at it by developing my powers of observation.

The acceleration in the rate of change is causing havoc. Specialization is necessary for survival, and increasingly the focus is narrowing because it's so hard to keep up with the knowledge and information in your field. There's little time to study the big picture and people increasingly feel lost. They want to see the world whole. That's the service I try to provide.

Everyone has a gift, a special talent in life. I was lucky to find mine. Many people never do. I'm a born synthesizer and teacher. My life's purpose is to learn and then to teach others. I have a talent for finding investment opportunities and articulating them to others, but making money is not my goal. It's striving to serve my clients with dedication, passion, and integrity. A true commitment to serve the needs of your clients is a powerful motivator and enormously satisfying. Along the way, I wrote five investment books, *Street Smart Investing* and *Is Inflation Ending? Are You Ready?* among them.

Money comes to me easily, but I was never attached to it. There's very little meaning to me in accumulating it. Perhaps I should tell you how I got started in business. I particularly remember the stock market bust of 1973–74 and the ensuing recession. None of the experts saw it coming. I came to the conclusion that the forecasting business was not dependable. As a consequence, I decided to study how the great investors made their fortunes. If you buy 5 percent of a public company, you must file a 13D statement with the Securities and Exchange Commission (SEC) within five business days. This is a mandatory securities law, but at the time no one was studying 13Ds; they were thrown into a big box in a back office at the SEC in Washington, D.C. I studied 13Ds over the course of a long time and amassed a large database on who was successful and who wasn't. I discovered Warren Buffett, Larry Tisch, Carl Icahn, Henry Singleton, and many others. Some of them had public companies, so there was a lot of information available on their investment philosophy and approach.

I decided I would research the companies they purchased and try to understand why they invested. In the late 1970s, the stock market was incredibly cheap and selling well below breakup value, which was the major driving force of many 13D filings. I piggybacked on several of these investments, which almost always worked out over time, particularly when the big investor acted as a catalyst.

In the spring of 1983, I decided to take my knowledge public. I wrote an eight-page summary describing the track record and philosophy of the major investors I had uncovered. I offered a subscription to a newsletter for $195 a year describing the activities of the great investors and my attempt to understand why they made their investments. I sent this letter to two hundred of my friends and acquaintances, and to my amazement I received a 50 percent response.

So with a $25 initial investment for postage and printing, I had 100 subscribers and a cash kitty of nearly $20,000. Shortly thereafter, Max Newton, who was a syndicated columnist writing for the *New York Post,* published an article about my newsletter. He received so many calls that a week later — to free up his phone — he wrote another article including my number. Within a few days, I had another 150 subscribers. About a month later, Jane Bryant Quinn, a well-known and successful syndicated financial columnist, also wrote an article about the newsletter. She included the subscription price for a three-month trial and my post office box. In those days I always picked up the mail, and I anxiously visited the post office every day to check the response. Two days later, nothing had happened. Three days, nothing. Four days, still nothing. On the fifth day, I went to the post office, looked inside the box, and saw a single slip of paper. My heart fell. I opened the box and there was a note requesting I visit the postmaster. I gave him the receipt. He went into the back and brought out a four-foot mailbag filled to the top. I took it back to my office and discovered it was full of checks, truly one of the great moments of my life. Barely two months after launching my newsletter, I had nearly a thousand subscribers.

A few weeks later, Geoff Smith, at the time assistant managing editor of *Forbes,* decided to write up my investment approach and my newsletter. He published a very favorable three-page article in *Forbes.* As he related the story, he was unable to answer his phone for two months, and the story generated a greater response than anything *Forbes* had seen for years. It may be hyperbole, but that's what he told me. In any event, *Forbes* was kind enough to forward all inquiries to me, and by mid-September I had two thousand subscribers. Around that time I raised my subscription fee to $250 a year. Six months later, a friend of mine from college who was an institutional research analyst advised me to produce a product for the professional market. Accordingly, I developed a prototype and mailed it out to my subscribers. To my amazement, I received a hundred responses. Clearly there were many institutions in my subscriber base. I successfully closed thirty of these clients at $15,000 a year, and my affiliated broker closed another twenty. So I had

$750,000 cash in the bank to actually hire the staff and launch the service. As they say, the rest is history.

What are the lessons from this surprising success in so short a period? If you have an original idea, it can do very well. Also, if the little things go right, you know you are on the right track. Finally, cash flow is all-important to a business. It's crucial for a start-up — indeed any business — to be self-financing and not be dependent on outside capital. I've seen many businesses fail because the financial markets dried up. In my case, I've always been self-financing, and I've always tested a new idea with the customers before investing any money. I've been amazed at the millions of dollars that have been spent on speculation rather than validation by the customer first. Over the years, our service evolved many times to capitalize on what I thought were the investment opportunities. We began studying bankruptcies and distressed securities in 1986. We shifted to emerging markets in the late 1980s. We went to Hong Kong in 1991, Germany in 1993, Brazil in early 1994, and came back to the United States in early 1995 and devoted our efforts to technology.

I have spent most of my career studying markets. As they are a reflection of mass psychology in action, they offer special insights into human nature. For many years, I was one of Wall Street's most prominent "contrarians" — looking for a consensus and then taking a contrary or opposite stance. It worked flawlessly until 1996, when I expected the bull market to end. I was one or two years too early, depending on what measure you use.

The lessons of markets are fascinating: every boom is followed by a bust, every bust is followed by a recovery. Crowd psychology often goes to extremes at both ends, and that's where it becomes most challenging and complex.

My mother's brother, Jim Hunt, had an outstanding career. He attended Yale and graduated from Harvard Business School in the depths of the Depression. He went to work for one of the most prominent investment banking firms, was a founder of the Office of Strategic Services (OSS) in World War II, joined the CIA at its founding after the war, and later became head of intelligence for Western Europe. Afterward he returned to the United States to a top position in U.S. counter-intelligence and worked with the gifted and controversial James Jesus Angleton. I spent many of my early summers around the leading figures of intelligence both in the United States and in England. My uncle said that the securities business and intelligence were the most interesting of all careers. It's all a question of judgment. Who do you believe? Who can you depend on for accurate information? What is disinformation, what's real? I have read many of the famous books on intelligence, particularly *Bodyguard of Lies* by Anthony Cave Brown. The title comes from a famous Churchill quote: "In wartime, the truth is so precious it must be protected by a bodyguard of lies."

When I was a young teenager, I learned that several hundred years ago everyone thought the earth was flat and the center of the universe. We consider such opinions to be ludicrous now. I often ask myself what firmly held belief we now have that will prove equally absurd to generations ahead of us. I strive to re-move all prejudices and biases from my thinking. It's not easy, and you have to really work at it. After a lifetime of experi-ence and discipline, I have learned to come to issues with an open mind and a determination to find all sides of the problem. The older I become and the more experience I have, the more I see how little I truly know and understand. Often I will say that I finally understand a complex issue, market irrationality, or some aspect of human nature, and then the theory blows up, and I feel terribly humbled. The hard part is to remain open to new ideas and not lose your bearing because you become too flexible.

I read six to eight hours a day. I'm a speed-reader and can finish several books a day. We receive daily information from Internet sources on dozens of subjects. I subscribe to numer-ous publications and magazines on a wide variety of topics. I'm interested in history and its lessons, technology, the human genome, the future, the meaning of life, eternal truths, true wisdom, genetic testing, immortality, life extension, new inventions and discoveries, biotechnology, nanotech, alternative medicine, spirituality, world religions, to name a few of the many topics that fascinate me. I recently began a series for my clients called "What I Learned This Week." It's been a useful way to record what I've learned on a wide variety of topics.

I describe my firm as a small intellectual commando unit that can shift direction at any moment — as soon as we discover opportunities. We are highly responsive to change. There have been ups and down, good and bad times, successes and failures, as well as stupidities. But I consider myself very lucky to have a career that I can practice while I'm deaf. This brings me to the next phase of my business life.

Wherever I look, I see mistrust in the business world — in other words, a lot of negative energy. Mistrust is everywhere.

One of my long-term goals in life is to help restore trust in business. I don't want to overrate my potential, but this may be one of my missions in life. As Victor Hugo said, "All the forces in the world are not so powerful as an idea whose time has come." I think "the time" is rapidly approaching. The world can't go on much longer with its present level of mistrust. You can see the havoc of mistrust everywhere: pervasive employment and marriage contracts, deceptions, accounting manipulation, fraud, greed, litigation, product recall, and price gouging during crises. A handshake and a verbal commitment aren't worth much unless they are accompanied by a huge legal document the lawyers fight over for weeks.

How do you create trust? It can't be faked, and it's not an "intellectual" choice. I believe it has to come from the heart. There is a true integrity about serving customers that is so absolute and powerful that customers automatically widen their level of trust. It's a cycle that feeds on itself and goes beyond pure business to a true awareness. When service becomes your primary focus, you can't help but make a profit. Business should start with service and let the profit take care of itself. That's how I began, and with every passing year I value the philosophy more. The only way to banish mistrust is to introduce true integrity and an open heart. If everyone were to successfully overcome their own personal issues with trust and mistrust, the world would change. You have to start somewhere, and it's up to each one of us. Will you help me on this journey?

25

Judge Not,
Lest Ye Be Judged

FRIENDS FALL IN AND OUT of your life. Some of them move away. Interests diverge. Some friends you knew only as a married couple. Some people don't grow at all; some develop in different ways from you. What you want and need in friends changes. And some die.

The friend I miss the most is Peter Banker, who died of a stroke in 1996. As time passes, I miss him more. I've rarely found his equal in true, unconditional friendship. I can give no better description of his character than this eulogy, which I delivered at his funeral:

True friendship is the rarest quality on earth. It is so hard to know if people befriend us because they care for us deeply or want something we can give. Is the friendship conditional on our health, our prosperity, our personal behavior, our station in life? Is the friendship unconditional and true? In Peter Banker you had an unconditional and true friend, no matter who you were.

Hemingway defined dignity as grace under pressure. Peter exemplified this quality. In the past ten years, he suffered a number of profound disappointments. Yet his courage never faltered. His spirit held firm. His dignity held fast. Peter's most endearing quality was his joy at his friends' success. Never a gleam of envy or jealousy in our Peter. The worse his luck, the more pleasure he took in the victories of his friends. How many times when I mentioned some small success of mine, Peter said, "that's terrific," with a voice full of enthusiasm and genuine happiness.

Peter and I must have played tennis a thousand times. And every time he heard of my workout schedule for that day, he'd tell me that I was his role model. But if the truth be known, Peter was my role model. He was a true gentleman in every sense of the word. His manners were impeccable. He treated women with more respect and kindness than any man I ever knew. No matter how provoked, I never heard him criticize anyone. I likened him often to Horatio at the bridge. No matter how many things went wrong, no matter how much stress he experienced or adversity he encountered, Peter faced his problems with unflinching courage. Even when a dear friend disappointed him, Peter couldn't bring himself to say a single word against that person. Once you were Peter's friend you were so for life — and unconditionally. I visited him the Friday before last, and even though he was in terrible pain, I saw the same brave, courageous Peter. Uncomplaining, even if he could have talked, dignified, even in the face of his massive, debilitating stroke. No one knows what lies on the other side. But for Peter there is now blissful peace. He leaves a legacy that will live on. His courage in the face of adversity, his innate dignity, his loyalty to friends have touched all of us deeply and profoundly. Rest peacefully, Peter. We will miss you always.

As I think about Peter, I ponder the quality of friendship and fair-weather friends compared to foul-weather ones. How many of the latter do we have and how many of the former? It's a good question to ask, because adversity can strike at any moment, and we might find we have been investing our time in the wrong places.

I've come to believe that friendship is all about positive energy. I think it's very hard to sustain a meaningful bond if there is criticism between friends. How many times have we listened to acquaintances gossiping in a negative way about their "friends"? As soon as you leave, do they talk the same way about *you*? A close friend recently commented that my hearing impediment causes me to miss important remarks that people make — remarks that are negative. She said if I could hear all that people say, I wouldn't see as much good in them as I do. A good point. But I suspect that, even if I could hear the many negative remarks people make, I would still see the positive side of them. I'm constantly making allowances for people and trying to understand the motivation behind negative or antagonistic behavior so that I can be compassionate toward them rather than angry at them.

Peter Drucker, one of the great "management" thinkers of the latter part of the twentieth century, believes you cannot build performance on weakness; you can build only on strength. He thinks the annual review process of companies, which focuses on what someone is doing wrong, is very destructive. You visit a marriage counselor. After the complaints by both sides are voiced, the counselor asks, "What do you love about him . . . about her?" You can't effect a reconciliation by focusing on the negatives. Constructive criticism is probably an oxymoron. If it's done at all, the better alternative is the so-called Socratic method, where you get someone to see the errors of their ways by asking them subtle questions, and because of the answers they give, they may eventually see the light. Or, at the very least, we should preface our "constructive criticism" with every conceivable positive we can think of.

This leads me to ponder how I have been perceived over the years. Because of my deafness, there may well have been considerable misunderstanding of who I am. My handicap may have distorted how I was perceived. What did people think when I looked intently at their lips instead of their eyes? What impression did I give when a smile was plastered on my face, no matter what the conversation? Did they perceive me as unfeeling, vacuous, uninterested, stupid? What about those people who asked me a question that I never heard? Did they see me as rude and uncooperative? During my times of enormous stress, tension, and loneliness, how did people see me? Did they take me at face value, or did they look beneath the surface?

When I received comments on this book, I learned that no one really knew what was going on inside me, not even my closest associates, my friends, my children, or my mother. We think we really know someone. But maybe we don't know that person at all! This made me think about people who have maladies or hidden traumas. Do I bring sufficient compassion and understanding to every human encounter? Am I seeing people in a positive or negative light? Maybe an angry friend has a beautiful heart but is dying on the inside from loneliness. Perhaps this irritable, nasty woman has deep sorrow she can't release, or hormone problems. Perhaps the selfish and inconsiderate couple is not really that way — only consumed with a personal health crisis. You never know until you see inside someone's heart.

I wonder what casual acquaintances will think when they read this book and see a different side of me. What about those who formed a superficial impression of me, which in light of new revelations is in error? What about those persons who — unknowingly — were insensitive? Will they now reevaluate how they judge people and how their opinions of others are formed? Will they become more open, less judgmental? Will they make different choices in the future? Will they open their hearts?

26

My Competitive Advantage

NOISE IS an unpleasant fact of life. It is a huge distraction and causes many people to lose their concentration and focus. Some call it noise pollution. I combat it with a simple tool. When flight attendants spend ten minutes announcing the gates of the connecting flights, I disconnect. When someone insults me, lectures me, or starts talking negatively about other people, I can tune out. When the conversation is boring, I can drift into another world. When a baby screams on an airplane, I can fade out. Airport loudspeakers, which often go nonstop, are particularly offensive. I usually turn my hearing aid off when I am in airports. No noise wakes me when I'm sleeping. I don't hear sirens, thunder, or the loud music from the children's rooms. If I need to concentrate on a book or an article, and there is a lot of background noise, I simply turn off the switch on my hearing aid.

There are also some serious advantages that offset some of my losses. First, consider my powers of concentration. In order to communicate with people, I have learned to develop a very intense focus. This serves me well in many other areas. I concentrate *totally* on one task until it's completed, or, if need be, I can move back and forth between various projects without losing a beat. This increases my personal productivity to a very high level. Focus and concentration are essential to completing any task, whether it's learning, making decisions, writing, thinking — or "hearing."

They say when you lose one sense, the other ones compensate. After three sinus operations and severe allergies, I have a poor sense of smell. My taste buds are desensitized, and I know I'll never be chosen to taste the quality of a winery's latest growth. I've also become more nearsighted over the last twenty years. I'm deaf. What's left? Hopefully, *something* improved. I think it was intuition — or, in my case, an ability to see and understand a person's *entire being,* a highly developed awareness.

Dostoevsky wrote that you know someone by that person's laugh. "If you wish to glimpse inside a human soul and get to know a man, don't bother analyzing his ways of being silent, of talking, of weeping, or seeing how much he is moved by noble ideas; you'll get better results if you just watch him laugh. If he laughs well, he's a good man."

Napoleon believed that your whole character shows on your face — but not until middle age, and until then, you'll know people best by understanding their motivations in life. I study the laughs, the smiles, and any signs of motivation I can pick up from people's faces. I am not judging them; I am trying to understand, with all the tools available to me, who they really are. I look into people's eyes — as they say, the windows of the soul — and learn a great deal about them. Are they happy, sad, shy, bitter, intelligent, sensitive, compassionate, world-weary, cynical, mean-spirited, repressed, at peace, full of conflicts, in pain, driven, compulsive, dogmatic, or judgmental? Are they strong, weak, self-pitying, on the emotional precipice? Are the eyes clear or cloudy? Are the eyes nervous, bulging, oversized, neurotic?

I learn from people's facial lines, the texture of the skin on their hands and on their neck, their muscular and vascular development, their fingernails and the lines on the palms of their hands. Do they take care of themselves physically? Do they sit still or fidget constantly, interrupting the answer to their own questions? Do they talk with hands on their chins, with fingers covering their mouth? Do they talk all the time or do they listen? And if they listen, do they *hear*? Do they ask questions about other people? Do they show a sincere interest in the people around them? I learn from the books — or lack of books — in their library, the magazines they read, what they talk about, whether they are positive or negative about friends. Do they sit far away from you on a sofa, watch you when you talk, listen to other conversations when you are talking to them? I watch the interaction of people, particularly married couples. Is there peace and tranquility between them, or is there tension? The signals of happiness, peace of mind, love, closeness *or* friction, bitterness, anger, lack of interest, and sexual dissatisfaction are all there. We merely have to look for them.

Henri Troyat wrote a magnificent biography of Leo Tolstoy. Near the end of the book, Troyat describes Tolstoy's unique awareness as he walks through a field — not an overturned blade of grass or an insect or a flower or any motion in nature failed to catch the novelist's attention. I certainly haven't reached that level of awareness, but all the thousands of hours I have spent with people, unable to hear a word they said, was employed productively — in learning as much as I could about human nature through observation. This awareness helps me in many ways. I'm sure I have a heightened sensitivity due to deafness — not only because of the loss and resulting struggle, but because it is nature's way of compensating me.

I'll tell you a secret. I learned this many years ago, forgot it, then relearned it. Here's my theory and my belief. There are not many men in this world who have more intuition than a woman. It's not even a contest. Whenever a wife, mother, sister, daughter, or lady friend offers advice on business, friends, potential partners, investments, child rearing, suitability of marriage partners, health habits, it may be prudent for us men to listen. I'm blessed because deafness made me depend on women most of my life. Their instincts are phenomenal, and I am constantly humbled. How can I mourn my loss, when I have gained so much?

27

I Count My Blessings

I N THE LATE 1980s, Oliver Sacks wrote a remarkable book
called *Seeing Voices: A Journey into the World of the Deaf.*
Sacks points out that a prelingually deaf child is unable to hear
his or her parents and with no grasp of language risks being re-
tarded. Sacks writes that the congenitally deaf "were considered
'dumb' (stupid) for thousands of years and were regarded . . . as
'incompetent' — to inherit property, to marry, to receive education, to have adequately challenging work — and were denied
fundamental human rights." Prior to 1750, according to Sacks,
the prelingually deaf were "treated by law in society as little
better than imbeciles."

I don't have to take you any farther down this road to illustrate how dramatically the life of a deaf person has improved.
I count my many blessings. I was born in the latter part of the
twentieth century, a true age of enlightenment. I live in the United
States of America, a great country which, despite its flaws, offers
opportunity of all kinds, unprecedented economic prosperity,
widespread education, transparency, the rule of law, the First
Amendment, *habeas corpus,* accountability, and unparalleled
health standards.

I am able to financially support myself in spite of a handicap.
I live in the era of cochlear implants. The Internet and e-mail
have opened up a huge new world of communication for the
hearing impaired. I went deaf long after I learned speech, so
I have no speech or learning impediment. I live in an age of
medical advances that truly boggle the mind. I live in a time

when women participate more fully in the economy than at any other time in history. There's never been a better time in world history to be handicapped.

I am in excellent health. I survived adversity and found meaning in my suffering. I live at a time when consciousness of the plight of late-deafened adults may be on the verge of changing. I sometimes joke that life is essentially logistics, statistics, and semantics. There is some truth to this. But on a more profound scale, the key word in life is "relative." By this I mean, look at your life relative to the past, relative to history, relative to others, and relative to your gains and your losses, weaknesses and strengths, triumphs and tragedies. I know where I stand, and the conclusion is that I'm extraordinarily blessed.

28

The Sound of Music

───────────
───

*For I speak to all men, in a language that all understand
... Even the deaf hear me, if they but listen to the voices of
their own souls.* — Allan C. Inman, *I Am Music*

PEOPLE ASK ME often about music. "Do you ever think about
music? Do you wish you could still hear it? Do you remember old songs? Can you still 'hear' in your memory the music
you once loved?"

I answer, "I never think about it."

"Why don't you take a trip back into your consciousness to
the joy you once had from music?"

"No," I say. "That would not be a trip of joy, but of sadness."

I grew up in a musical household. My mother was a pianist,
then a composer, and later for twenty-five years wrote record
reviews of classical music. I grew up living with Beethoven, Bach,
Mozart, and Chopin. Music is inspirational. It deeply affects
your mood. Music makes you happy or sad. It reaches you on
a different level from reading and talking and seeing. I've cried
listening to music. Music inspires me to do noble deeds.

My mother has very painful arthritis and has been unable to
play the piano for many years. She keeps an old, beaten up,
untuned piano in a cabin next to her cottage in the mountains.
I recently suggested we give the piano away because the room
was cluttered. "I'll never live without a piano in my house!"
she said. That says a lot about how much we love music in our
family. Of course, I didn't have my mother's musical talents,

even when I heard well. In fact, my musical career peaked at age fourteen when I took saxophone lessons from a very pretty girl my own age.

Do I miss music? I'm sure I do, but I simply don't think about it. I don't mourn my loss, and I keep all my feelings for music under very tight control. I might lapse into nostalgia occasionally, but not for long. What good will it do to brood over a part of my life that I can never recover? My favorite piece of music is Beethoven's Ninth Symphony. I first heard it around the age of six or seven and it was so beautiful that I felt my heart breaking in two. Music sounds to me now like noise. I can't distinguish the intricate sounds, the high and lows, the individual instruments. It's like using a sledgehammer instead of the surgeon's scalpel or the diamond cutter's finest instruments. I may have an emotional block about music because I loved it so much. But so far I haven't wanted to force myself to face it because I know there's no chance of ever really hearing music again.

I *can* hear the rhythm of music, and I am able to dance. In fact, I love dancing and derive huge pleasure from it. I'm the first one on the dance floor, and the last to leave.

I wonder how many hearing people are fully aware of how much late-deafened adults miss music. Let me tell you a story. A few years ago, I met an interesting woman. She was attractive and smart, and there seemed a basis for a relationship. One day she talked to me about music and how much it meant to her. She complained that I never played music in my house. Then, she said, "I don't think I could have a relationship with a man who wasn't able to appreciate music." Did she mean that she couldn't have a relationship with a man who didn't love music? Or, did she mean that she couldn't have a relationship with a man who was no longer able to appreciate music? I never asked her and I wonder if she understands the difference.

29

My Life's Epiphany

N THE SPRING OF 1995, I couldn't hear my own voice, and I knew it was time to act. I could no longer wait for hair cell rejuvenation. So I decided it was time for a cochlear implant, a form of bionic ear. They surgically implant electrodes in your head, which stimulate the brain directly. You must learn to process speech all over again, which can take a long time, depending on the person.

Cochlear implants work only for certain people. I had a big file on cochlear implants. A compassionate doctor in Boston researched the pros and cons of the procedure for me and gave me thumbs up. I chose Dr. Noel Cohen of NYU Medical, who's the number one cochlear implant surgeon in the world, or so I have been told. When it's your brain, who wants second best? Dr. Cohen is the kindest, warmest surgeon I've ever met. He puts you at ease and answers all your questions, a rarity in his profession.

But first, I had to have tests to determine if I was a proper candidate for the procedure. Betsy Bromberg is my audiologist, and she has the patience of Job and the biggest heart in her profession. I had many tests over many months, and I found I'm a candidate. The surgery was scheduled for October 1996. My closest friends were very optimistic. I got letters, cards, and faxes from people who told me the surgery will change my life. After years of loss and disappointment, I was reluctant to hope. I believed I was not hoping, but as it turns out I was.

Dr. Cohen advises me to have the surgery in my "good" ear, in other words, the "hearing" ear. I'm scared — the surgery is irreversible, and the little hearing in this ear will be destroyed. But I follow Dr. Cohen's advice, rubbing my lucky stones. Incredibly, my health plan, sponsored by Aetna, pays for the entire $50,000 cost. I'm only $500 out of pocket.

After the surgery, six weeks pass before I am "hooked up" and the implant operates. So now, as I wait, I'm totally and absolutely, stone deaf. I cannot hear the slightest sound, even the blast of a jet engine. I travel to a friend's wedding in San Francisco. I don't know anyone except the groom. My comprehension is at rock bottom, but not much worse than before the hearing in the right ear was destroyed. I am now seeing the worst and I know I can live with it. From here on, things can only get better.

Dr. Cohen hooks up the implant. I go out to dinner the next night with two of my closest friends. "What does it sound like?" they ask.

I answer, "A castrated boy on fast forward, superimposed on a police squawk box. All of that — for *this*?" I say.

Yet as the days pass, I begin to comprehend more. Speech sounds more normal, but I no longer have a reference point because it's been so many years since I could hear. The years now fall away. I hear as I did in 1994, then 1993, then 1992, then 1990, and then 1988. My comprehension goes from zero to as high as 85 percent in an absolutely quiet setting, and almost 100 percent with lipreading. Of course, the left ear is still totally deaf. I can now talk on the phone. I do not comprehend everything but enough to carry on a complete conversation with many people — most important, with the people I love. I feel like a prisoner released after ten years of solitude. As my freedom comes, my spirits soar. Now I can once again hear the love sounds of my lover at night. I still can't hear music, but a woman making love to me is the gentlest, most beautiful music in the world.

It is said that getting your hearing back is more stressful than losing it. There is some truth to this. I hear new sounds that I haven't heard for years. The noise itself almost drives me crazy.

The fax machine sounds like a shrieking banshee, and I have to leave the room when a fax comes in, which is frequent.

It's now Thanksgiving of 1996. I'm in Sun Valley with my daughter and mother. We are spending the holidays with Jack and Angela Hemingway. Jack has a big mustache and he mumbles, a devastating combination. I say to Jack: "All these years, I never heard a word you said."

"Yes, I know. It's been very frustrating for me."

"Now, I can hear you."

So we make up for lost time. As the evening progresses, I come to know Jack Hemingway as he is, an exciting revelation for me. I ask if he remembers his father's short story, "In Another Country." The young Nick Adams is injured in World War I and is in physical therapy. He meets an Italian major, the finest swordsman in Italy, whose hand is mangled and who recently lost the beautiful wife he adored.

The Italian says to Nick Adams: "If he is to lose everything, he should not place himself in a position to lose that [his wife]. He should not place himself in a position to lose. He should find things he cannot lose."

I tell Jack that I read the story when I was fourteen and it made a huge impression on me. It was a philosophy worth adopting, although life played a trick on me — as it does on all of us.

Then, I realize something profound, my life's epiphany, if you will. I realize that one-on-one conversations, like this, mean more to me than anything else in the world. This gift was taken away from me. Then given back.

30

The Struggle Isn't Over, but the Mission Begins

THE COCHLEAR IMPLANT is one of the greatest advances in medicine. I don't want to belittle other scientific miracles, but for a deaf person, the cochlear implant truly restores life. In a perfect setting, with a cooperative companion, and using lipreading, I can understand nearly 100 percent of what is said. I am able to talk on the telephone with friends and loved ones. I have a new "smart" cellular phone with which I can actually converse reasonably fluently with people on a portable phone.

Stress and isolation have been drastically reduced. I can pick up a phone and reach out to anyone on the spur of the moment. I can sometimes hear what people say to me without lipreading if they are very near to my right, "hearing" ear and they speak slowly and enunciate carefully. I am now more comfortable at business presentations because the room is usually quiet, and, generally, I can hear most questions. The release of tension and the major reduction in stress have dramatically improved my interaction with people.

There are still limitations, but I almost never think of them. I'm still deaf in my left ear. I can't hear loudspeaker or microphone announcements of any kind. I cannot hear what's being said in noisy environments. I don't comprehend people with foreign accents. I still depend heavily on lipreading. Enunciation, speaking slowly, and voice projection are still crucial elements in my comprehension. I still can't follow group conversation.

My hearing — and all my possessions, everything I have — belongs to God. God took my hearing away and then chose to partially restore it. This is the most profound gift I have ever received, and no matter how grateful I am, it would never do justice to this miracle of a life reborn.

Now comes the mission. God has asked me to tell my story and describe my journey. That is all that matters now — the mission to serve the handicapped and the lonely people with hidden wounds and sorrows, and to follow His guidance as I fulfill His will.

31

How Deafness
Changed My Life

Do *what thy manhood bids thee do, from none but self
expect applause;*
He *noblest lives and noblest dies who makes and keeps his
self-made laws.*

—Sir Richard Burton, *The Kasidah: Of Haji Abdu El-Yezdi*

I TRAVEL ALONG the journey of life. Do I make a difference? Do
I pass through unnoticed, having no impact and with no one
caring when I die? Do I grow as a human being? Do I become a
better person? Do I max out my potential? Am I a good father,
son, and husband? Am I a loyal and dependable friend? How
can I improve myself? What am I really like? As I think I am, or
do others see me differently? Am I too shy, too emotional, too
defensive, too aggressive? Do I listen to constructive criticism?
Am I too hard on myself? Too easy? Too quick to anger, too
quick to forgive and forget?

I am an introspective person, perhaps due to my nature and
because I am alone so much. So I ask these questions. My father believed that Freudian analysis was very destructive to U.S.
society because psychoanalysis made people look inward. I was
indoctrinated with my father's philosophy and I agree with it.
If you dwell on yourself too much, your loss, your pain, you
will have a very hard time overcoming it or healing. You have

to let go. The great challenge for me as a late-deafened adult is to forget my loss, to dwell on what I have, not on what I don't!

I don't underestimate the contribution of my friends and family members, but the reality is that I faced deafness by myself. And, of course, that's the way it must be in the end. It's how you deal with a personal crisis that determines the outcome. Others can offer emotional support, love, and sensitivity. But it is up to you to change how you feel.

In the summer of 2001, I was having dinner with Judy Biggs and her husband at the Evergreen restaurant in Ketchum, Idaho. A life-threatening virus had attacked Judy several years before. For a period she could barely walk, and her nervous system was in acute jeopardy. She had a very active life, with an even more active husband whom she loved to accompany on climbing expeditions all over the world.

"You are so happy here," I said. "Sun Valley really agrees with you. You should spend more time here."

"It's been a psychological adjustment for me. I guess I've come out the other side. Now that I can walk better, I don't think of what I'm missing. I think of how lucky I am to be walking at all."

That is an attitude that I admire greatly, and I couldn't express it better.

I think I am one of the luckiest people in the world. To me, life is so beautiful that it sometimes leaves me speechless. I am now confident that I can handle almost every adversity. When you've gone deaf and accepted it, there's not too much more life can throw at you that you can't handle.

Life is wonderful! I've been saying this for years. Friends argue with me and say, "Life is good *some* of the time."

But my enthusiasm is contagious. Now when I say life is wonderful, they answer, "Yes, life *is* wonderful!"

I frequently visit one of the best restaurants in New York State, which is located about a two-hour drive from Manhattan. The proprietor is called Orlando. He and his wife are Europeans with enormous sensitivity and artistic passion. Both of Orlando's parents were deaf, but all five of their children hear perfectly. He is an artist, not a businessman.

In the spring of 1996, I was in Orlando's private dining room with five of my closest friends. I was reading Peter Banker's eulogy, crying. Orlando heard parts of this eulogy and saw my grief. Two days later, Orlando called me. He apologized profusely. He said he barely knew me, but his wife insisted that he call me.

"I'm honored you called me. Thank you for calling me," I said.

After twenty minutes of apologizing and my continuing encouragement, Orlando stated the reason for his call: "I want to kill myself."

Business had turned bad. He had mortgaged the restaurant and was overleveraged because of the purchase of a retirement home. I canceled my plans for the evening and went to his restaurant for dinner that night. After everyone left, we sat down to talk. I listened to him for several hours. Then I said, "What are the good things in your life?" We wrote them down on a yellow pad. Quickly, it became apparent there was a lot to live for.

He called me two weeks later: "You saved my life." Like the Native Americans who have permanent responsibility for someone they rescue, I am responsible for Orlando. I love him and make a special trip to his restaurant several times a year.

In August 1999 I returned from a trip to Tibet. Shortly afterward, I visited Dr. Ross, a wise and talented ear, nose, and throat doctor. I told him of my trip, and he discussed his two visits to Nepal. I invited him for dinner to show me his slides and to share with him my pictures of Tibet. His wife was sick, and so he brought his daughter-in-law.

I also invited another woman who has suffered greatly in her life. When I was leaving Sun Valley on my way to Tibet, we were not only on the same plane but were seated next to each other. She was on her way to a wedding in Aspen, which the Dalai Lama was expected to attend. This was too much of a coincidence, and I felt she should join us.

The four of us sat down to dinner. I asked Dr. Ross to tell us about himself. "My father left my mother for his secretary when I was eight. I didn't see him again for twenty-eight years." We talked about what kind of an effect that experience had on his life. Then, I turned to the daughter-in-law and asked about her. It was clear she was close to breaking down, so we changed the subject for a few minutes. Then, I turned back to her and inquired about her childhood. She started to cry. "My mother died when I was eight years old. All the love went out of my life because my father was hard and mean."

I took hold of her hand and all four of us cried for fifteen minutes, saying not a word, holding each other's hands. Strangers cry in my house all the time. I hold their hands, hug them, and tell them it's fine to cry. These experiences are the best and most powerful of my entire life. I never forget them, and they provide my strongest reason for living.

Thank you, dear God, for showing me that suffering leads to growth, which leads to compassion and love. Now I hear the sounds of sorrow and loneliness and grief — like I never did before.

32

The Indescribable Power of Love and Gratitude

─────────────

Out of desire to help as many people as possible remain or become healthy, I had worked for years taking care of the sick. And the more afflicted people that I see, the more I become convinced that illness is not just an individual problem, but a result of the deformation of society as a whole.

Unless something is done about the deformed world that we live in, and unless we can heal the wounded soul, the number of people suffering from physical illnesses will not decline....

Just as a drop in a pond creates a ripple that spreads out endlessly, the deformity of even one soul spreads throughout the world, resulting in global deformities.

—Dr. Masaru Emoto, *The Hidden Messages in Water*

D R. MASARU EMOTO, an internationally renowned Japanese scientist, has done very original research on how molecules of water are affected by our thoughts, words, and feelings. The importance of water is often forgotten. A fetus is made up of 99 percent water. When we are born our bodies are 90 percent water. By the time we reach adulthood, the water content has declined to 70 percent, and by the time we die, our bodies will contain only about 50 percent water. Each day the human liver filters nearly 200 liters of water for delivery to the other organs in the body. In other words, throughout most of our lives, we are mostly water.

Dr. Emoto has written a fascinating book entitled *The Hidden Messages in Water*. He explains how crystals formed in frozen water reveal changes, when specific concentrated thoughts are directed toward them. Emoto studied and photographed crystals in water. These crystals are created during a twenty-to-thirty-second period when ice begins to melt. Emoto's pictures of crystals have become world famous. *The Hidden Messages in Water* has sold four hundred thousand copies, largely through word of mouth. He has lectured in many countries all over the world, and people are deeply moved by his photographs of ice crystals. As Emoto relates, "I often hear people gasp in surprise and sometimes even see them shed tears. I have discovered that a single drop of water can have various ripple effects on an individual."

Emoto found that the water of Tokyo, which is heavily chlorinated, did not contain a single complete crystal. Apparently, the chlorine totally destroyed the structure found in natural water. Exposing water to music created amazing results. When Beethoven's Pastoral Symphony, with its bright and clear tones, was played to water, beautiful and well-formed crystals were created. Mozart's Fortieth Symphony, a prayer to beauty, made crystals that were delicate and elegant. But when the water was exposed to violent heavy-metal music, the crystals were fragmented and malformed at best.

Other experiments were equally extraordinary. Emoto wrote phrases on pieces of paper and wrapped the paper around bottles of water with the words facing inward. "The results of the experiment didn't disappoint us. Water exposed to 'Thank You' formed beautiful hexagonal crystals, but water exposed to the word 'Fool' produced crystals like the ones formed when the water was exposed to violent heavy-metal music." The author concluded there was an important lesson: "The vibrations of good words have a positive effect on our world, but the vibrations from negative words have the power to destroy." Of all the crystals the author photographed, the most beautiful was the one created from the words "love" and "gratitude."

Emoto believes that ice crystals are closely linked to the human soul. As he pondered why his photographs moved so many people, Emoto came to believe that ice crystals contain the key to the mysteries of the universe. "This key can unlock the consciousness required to understand the proper order of the universe and our role in it."

It is well known that all human beings vibrate at different frequencies. For example, someone carrying great sadness will send a sadness frequency. A person who is full of joy and loves life will convey that frequency. But a person who acts with evil intentions will send off dark frequencies. "The fact that everything is in a state of vibration also means that everything is creating sounds." So water, which is so pervasive in the human body, is sensitive to the frequencies being transmitted across the world — essentially reflecting the frequencies themselves. If you fill your heart with love and gratitude, you will be surrounded by the same emotions, but if you send out negative energy, full of hate and dissatisfaction and sadness, you will find yourself in exactly that world.

A family that subscribes to a magazine that Dr. Emoto publishes conducted a remarkable experiment. They put rice in two glass jars, and every day for a month they said "thank you" to one jar and "you fool" to the other. After a month, the rice that was the recipient of "thank you" started to ferment with a mellow smell of malt. The rice that was blasted with the message "you fool" rotted and turned black. This experiment was eventually conducted by hundreds of families throughout Japan, and all of them reported the same results. One family tried an interesting variation. They said "thank you" to one bottle of rice, "you fool" to the second bottle, and they simply ignored the third bottle. The rice that was ignored rotted before the rice that was exposed to "you fool." Emoto concluded that the most damaging form of human behavior is withholding attention.

Emoto also discusses negative emotions and how to dispel them. A few years ago, a university in Japan created a way of erasing sound with sound. The university made one noise that would erase the unwanted noise, thereby creating a quiet space (for example, around a public telephone). This same method has also been used to reduce the noise of an automobile engine. The same principle applies to human emotions. Every negative emotion has its opposite:

Hate	→	Gratitude
Anger	→	Kindness
Fear	→	Courage
Anxiety	→	Peace of Mind
Pressure	→	Presence of Mind

"If you've been made sick by the emotion of hate, then you need to look for healing in the emotion of appreciation."

Emoto also made another remarkable discovery. While love can have enormous healing powers, the combination of love and gratitude is exceedingly more powerful. Emoto experimented with two types of water, (1) distilled water and (2) tap water exposed to the words "love" and "gratitude." The crystals created from the distilled water were deformed and incomplete. But the normally formless tap water, when exposed to the words "love" and "gratitude," made complete crystals. The words "love" and "gratitude" were able to make the water immune to the negative effects of chlorine.

Emoto carries his thesis even further: gratitude is more powerful than love. Emoto found that the love *and* gratitude crystals resemble gratitude crystals more than the love crystals. "What this indicates is that the gratitude vibration is more powerful and has a greater influence. Love tends to be a more active energy, the act of giving oneself unconditionally. By contrast, gratitude is a more passive energy, a feeling that results from having been given something — knowing that you have been given the gift of life and reaching out to receive it joyously with both hands." The author suggests having twice as much gratitude as love.

33

My Transformation

The quality of mercy is not strain'd.
It droppeth as the gentle rain from heaven
Upon the place beneath: it is twice blest;
It blesseth him that gives and him that takes.
—William Shakespeare, *The Merchant of Venice*

HOW DID YOU MAKE the transformation from negative to positive? How did you avoid getting caught up in negative adversity? Explain to us how you did it, how you survived. Tell us about the movement of energy from negative to positive. Tell us about your loss compared with your gain. These are important questions, the most difficult I face in writing this book.

Let me begin by telling two stories. I was skiing in Vail over Thanksgiving vacation of 1990 with two very close female friends. We spent much of the night talking about life and spiritual happiness. My friends held my hands, and one of them said, "Kiril, look in the mirror and say that you love yourself." Not only was I unable to look in the mirror, but I most certainly could not say that I loved myself.

You can't make a transformation until you love yourself. When you start seeing all your weaknesses, mistakes, and stupidities with compassion and love and forgiveness, you are on the way to being transformed. I love myself now. Sometimes I'll look at myself in the mirror and say, "What a nice guy! What a sweet, wonderful fellow you are. You are a really good person!" And I believe it's true!

The events of the other story occurred about two years later. After my divorce I went through seven years of intense self-analysis. I shared the responsibility for the failed marriage, and I wanted to learn about my faults and correct them before I married again and committed myself for life. This was a very painful and difficult process. It may seem to contradict what I said earlier about focusing outward, but I believe that you can't grow until you face a certain number of personal issues. If you want to learn from a failure, it seems to me, you have to analyze it a dozen different ways.

A friend advised me to visit a counselor who runs a spiritual healing center. The man was in his seventies and suffered enormously in concentration camps during World War II. Reportedly, his first wife committed suicide after he left her for another woman. This counselor was going away for the summer, and so I would have only one short meeting. I organized all my thoughts, history, and pertinent information to discuss with him. He listened to me for almost the entire session and then made a few remarks. The most memorable comment he made was that I needed to put an emotional wall around myself to keep certain people from hurting me. The session was over, and I drove into New York City for a meeting. On my way home, I drove past his house, and as I did, I had the strongest physiological experience of my life: A dam of accumulated tension burst in my stomach, and for days and weeks afterward I felt waves of relief and release that shook my whole body, my entire being, right from my heart to my soul. For the first time in my life, I didn't analyze. I let myself feel without thinking. This was an important step for me, as it is for anyone who thinks too much or who has led a life of control, whether by oneself or by others.

This eventually led to the point where I let myself feel the full extent of my pain. We should be rewarded for taking such courageous action, but the first emotion you feel is unbearable pain. The reward comes later.

Let me tell you about the day I hit bottom. I was walking along the streets of New York City. I was on the edge of an abyss — a black horrible abyss, which was on the verge of dragging me downward in an endless spiral. I desperately missed my wife and my family. I wasn't happy with myself. I was racked with guilt over my family's pain. I was burnt out and stressed out beyond reason from the effort to communicate. Everything looked black. I knew I had to save myself. I needed a new environment, a change of scene, a different place to live. I had to leave old memories and sorrows behind.

The impediments were huge: two children in school with life-long friends, a house, a business, an office, an elderly mother. Day by day, week by week, month by month, each impediment fell by the wayside. Perhaps it was written!

How did I make the transition from negative to positive? I did it in the following ways:

- I control my environment to favor my handicap.

- I avoid stress wherever and whenever possible.

- I surround myself with positive people and loved ones.

- I think positive thoughts.

- I love life.

- I find what I am good at and then do it.

- I don't waste much time anymore trying to correct my character flaws. It requires a negative focus, which I prefer to avoid.

- I accept there are limitations to everything — all good times end, including wonderful summers, life itself, the lives of our loved ones, and economic and stock market booms.

- I'm incredibly grateful for what I have.

Any transformation involves finding a way to view almost every event in a positive light. I know this sounds complicated — but it isn't. How do you take a hurtful, scary, or negative event and turn it into a positive? Does this require training, discipline, a good heart, spiritual development? There's an easy answer.

When I went deaf, I learned not to focus on losing the most important thing in my life. I closed the book of one-on-one conversations, put it on a shelf in the library, shut the door, locked it, and threw away the key. I turned away from that book and library and never looked back. You can't heal or grow if you hold on to grief or loss.

Also, when you are pushed beyond what you think you can handle, you must find a way to sleep. Anxiety breeds sleepless nights, which breeds stress. You have to sleep any way you can for as long and as often as you can. You can't make an emotional or spiritual transformation when you are exhausted. I can tell you that before my transformation, I went to bed hundreds of nights feeling depressed, lonely, sad, and isolated, and the next morning, after a deep sleep, I awoke and felt like a different person.

The second step is to throw yourself into an activity that you enjoy and believe in. Many people have written about working eighteen hours a day to deal with the loss of a spouse or parent or child. In my case, I took up biking, the best stress reliever I've ever found. I biked every day — rain, snow, heat, and cold. I was known to bike for four hours straight, even when the temperature was twenty degrees below zero. I love biking. It's a refuge, a way to relieve stress and to push your body. I biked two hundred miles a week for ten years.

My real transformation took place when I came to understand that deafness was God's greatest gift to me. When I stopped fighting and accepted God's will, and my condition, I found great inner peace. This, of course, is one of the essential messages of His Holiness the Dalai Lama, who has honored me greatly by writing a foreword to this book. In August 1999 I traveled to Tibet, which was one of the most memorable journeys of my life. Tibet is called "the roof of the world." The Tibetan plateau is higher than most of the world's mountains. Lhasa, located at twelve thousand feet above sea level, is the capital of Tibet and where the Potala Palace (the winter residence of the Dalai Lama before he was forced into exile in 1959) is located. The Tibetan people are what one might wish for the rest of humanity — gentle, kind, compassionate, tender, infinitely forgiving, and against all violence and killing of any kind. I spent entire days talking to Tibetans and came to know them well and to understand their suffering. Tibet is one of the most beautiful countries in the world, and for most of its life was the most isolated.

Immediately after returning from Tibet, I read every book that I could find about the Dalai Lama, by him, or about Tibet. It was a profound and moving experience. Tibetan Buddhism is one of the most complex and profound religions. Its practitioners seek enlightenment. Once you start on this path toward enlightenment, everything else seems unimportant by comparison.

My fascination with Tibetan culture and my desire to help preserve it eventually led me to become involved with Dr. Lobsang Sangay, a Ph.D. from Harvard Law School and a research fellow at the East Asian Legal Studies program of the Harvard Law School. Dr. Sangay lectures widely across the United States on Tibetan culture and the major issues facing the country. I have been honored to sponsor his studies and his continued presence at Harvard University.

After the Pope the Dalai Lama is the most recognized name on the planet. The reason is very simple. The world is in desperate need of spirituality, enlightenment, and the message of compassion that the Dalai Lama embodies. One of the best books ever written about the Dalai Lama is *In Exile from the Land of Snows* by John F. Avedon. The book recounts a pilgrimage in 1981 by the Dalai Lama to the holiest sites of Buddhism, where the author observed the Dalai Lama's meditation practices. Avedon writes: "[The Dalai Lama's] constant theme is that the essence of a Buddhist life lies in a person's own effort to purify the mind. By replacing its coarse, deluded states such as anger, attachment, and ignorance with their opposites, patience, equanimity, and wisdom, a lasting internal happiness can be achieved, independent of external conditions."

Every morning when the Dalai Lama wakes up at 3:30 a.m., his first thoughts are of the Buddha and his teaching of compassion and the interdependence of all things. By forgiving your enemies, the Dalai Lama believes, you progress more rapidly toward enlightenment.

Thanks to my friend Dick Strong, I was invited to meet His Holiness. Our private audience was arranged months in advance — by the most amazing coincidence — for September 19, 2001, only eight days after the terrorist attack on the World Trade Center. Our meeting with the Dalai Lama took place in Dharamsala, India, the headquarters of the Tibetan Government-in-Exile, forty miles from the Pakistan border. Many people in our group were emotionally distraught after the trauma of September 11, and they cried openly during our meeting with His Holiness. In my own case, after having seen *evil* in its rawist and ugliest form, a private audience with one of the most profoundly *good* men in the world gave me a powerful and unforgettable healing.

For the six months before my meeting with His Holiness, I pondered at great length what questions to ask him. But it was my son, Jay, who came up with the best question: "What is mankind most desperately in need of?" The Dalai Lama spent considerable time answering the question. He said that people rush after money, power, possessions, influence, and beauty, thinking these things will make them happy. But in reality everyone is seeking the same thing — peace of mind — but they can't seem to find it. His Holiness repeated these words over and over again: "peace of mind...peace of mind...peace of mind...peace of mind." The words still resonate in my consciousness.

I asked His Holiness to explain his personal interpretation of compassion. He said that a Tibetan had been kept prisoner in China for twenty years. Upon his release, he came to see the Dalai Lama in Dharamsala. The Tibetan told His Holiness that he became afraid while in prison.

"What were you afraid of?" asked the Dalai Lama.

"That I might lose my compassion for my Chinese jailers."

There was a young man accompanying us who filmed our session with the Dalai Lama. It was his turn to ask a question. He choked up with emotion and was unable to speak for a minute or more. He finally said, "*Why?* . . . I don't understand why they did it."

The Dalai Lama answered that there are mischievous and evil people in the world. They have highly developed intelligence, but their hearts remain cold. He continued, "We have to work on developing the heart."

So perhaps switching from negative to positive is really a development of the heart. As you make the transition from negative to positive thoughts, there are sure to be setbacks. But I have found that as the years pass by, I have almost entirely eliminated negative thoughts. Now only positive thoughts guide my life and emotions. I have learned to focus my positive energy like a laser, with all my being energized to make good things happen. One example of this was a vision I had in early 2003: how to help restore trust to the corporate world. As I wrote earlier, over the course of many years, trust between large corporations and their customers has declined drastically: there have increasingly been corporate scandals, recalled products, stonewalling by company lawyers, a lack of transparency, insensitivity to social problems and the environment, blatant greed, and an excessive focus on profits at the expense of serving the customer.

I envisioned inviting His Holiness to meet a group of our country's major CEOs and their spouses. Hopefully, intimate interaction between the Dalai Lama and these executives might help change the energy on the planet. My goal was totally selfless, only wishing for the betterment of humanity. I focused on this vision intensely, imagining it happening in very clear detail. From the moment I first conceived of the vision, I knew the event would take place. I never had a single doubt or a single worry. The universe had decided and I was merely a conduit.

In September 2004 I took a very good friend who is the founder of a very large and successful global business to a private audience with the Dalai Lama in Ft. Lauderdale, Florida. We spent almost two hours with His Holiness. Later, I heard from my friend's wife that this audience had been a "life-changing" event for her husband. In subsequent conversations my friend told me that the Dalai Lama had become part of his life on a daily basis, affecting his relationship with employees, contractors, and associates. In public speeches, my friend now frequently refers to the Dalai Lama and suggests that his message of compassion and peace of mind should be part of every executive's life. This was a great validation of my vision.

In early January 2005 His Holiness honored me enormously by agreeing to come to Sun Valley for four days to meet with national political figures and top corporate executives. As this book is published, the event has not yet occurred. So I cannot tell you the outcome. But with the universe opening the doors, everything is possible.

Tibetan Buddhism exerts a more profound influence on my life with each passing month. I am increasingly devoting my life to helping people make a transformation and heal their hidden sorrows. I do this as I did it: by showing them how to love themselves through compassion.

Meditation is a vital aspect of every day. I meditate before sleeping and after I awake in the morning. I also meditate after work and cleanse my mind of any negative thoughts or occurrences that took place during the day or the past week. I often visualize myself lying on the beach, with my toes facing the ocean. As the waves pass over me, they bring fresh and powerful new energy, and they wash away the old and stale thoughts.

On the advice of Tenzin Dhonden, a Tibetan lama born in Dharamsala who is my spiritual brother and is close to His Holiness, my meditation in the morning and at night is focused on losing consciousness and thereby passing into another consciousness. Tenzin calls this the highest form of meditation. Being able to stop the mind from thinking brings a glorious inner peace and reduces deep-seated stress. Most important, such meditation puts you in touch with your inner self, and as that occurs you learn to focus positive energy, and, in the words of Tenzin, "a stone wall is created in front of you to deflect all negative energy." My late-afternoon meditation is centered on expressing gratitude and love for the universe. I can feel strength and power coming into me and I know that all things are possible.

I also strive to avoid taking life personally. If you can detach yourself from the outcome, you won't be disappointed if your future does not materialize as you have dreamed it should. Sometimes I can literally see myself watching myself — in other words, one step removed from the feelings of Kiril Sokoloff. If you are unattached to the outcome, you can still strive mightily for victory but not be crushed at defeat or loss. Whatever happens is the will of God.

The more open your heart becomes, the easier it is to give and receive love. As I was transformed, I realized how many people I love! As I say, my heart bursts with love. I also love:

Sunsets, sunrises, the stars on a clear night...

Profound and moving books and paintings and statues...

The way the leaves sparkle in the wind on an autumn day...

The way my daughter's eyes light up with love when she says she loves me...

The way my son's eyes mist over when he hugs me and says goodbye...

The way the ocean pounds the shore with its primitive, elemental force...

The joy that comes from making a close bond and connection with another person...

The graceful red fox that leaps around the back of my property...

The way a lake sparkles on a sunny day...

The joy that comes from giving...

Leonard Bernstein conducting the "Ode to Joy" when the Berlin Wall falls, tears streaming down his face . . .

The way the snow feels under my skis on the first run of the day, when the sky is so blue it breaks your heart and the snow crystals sparkle . . .

Reading *Birdsong,* managing only twenty pages at a clip, walking down the corridor, my head knocking on the walls at the sheer beauty of Sebastian Faulks's writing . . .

Falling on my knees before sleep, overwhelmed by God's miracles and kindness to me . . .

Watching the flowers bloom and the majesty of nature's colors . . .

Seeing the gentle ripples of a late summer's river flowing quietly through the forest, a silver sheen reflecting off its surface . . .

Playing a hard-fought tennis match against superior opponents and not caring who wins, because we all play our best . . .

Triumphing over negative impulses and doing the right thing . . .

Unable to leave the house early in the morning without my four-year-old son waking up, holding my hand all the way to the car, waving goodbye down the driveway, onto the main road, my heart wrenched to leave his love . . .

Driving six hours in the car, my now eight-year-old son hugging me and kissing me the whole way, saying over and over again: "I love you, D. I love you, D. I love you, D." . . .

Driving home from work, my spirits soaring with excitement, accelerating up the steep highway, turning onto the dirt road, pulling up to our house, my wife shouting, "Daddy's home!" and my two beloved children running from wherever they are to hug me and love me . . .

Brushing my ten-year-old daughter's hair a thousand strokes a night and watching the texture glisten and shine and see her face light up with joy and love...

Telling her bedtime stories every night, where the Abominable Snowman or the Cookie Monster kidnaps her school bus, but not for long — because my daughter is the heroine, and she rescues everyone...

My beloved children tucked into sleeping bags on my bedroom floor because they can't bear to be separated from me (and my tears blot this page, as I write this and remember their love and our closeness and the indescribable pain of a broken family that loves each other with all their hearts)...

Having an unforgettable conversation (discovering Jack Hemingway for the first time or hearing Allyn Stewart say, "If you say it, I believe you")...

Remembering in my distant memory what music was like, recalling the last concert I went to, Judy Collins solo at Carnegie Hall, no orchestra, no piano, just her magnificent voice...

Waking up in the middle of the night and caressing the woman I love...

Waking up in the middle of the night — alone — and realizing that sleeping with your lover is one of God's greatest gifts...

Telling someone you love them and seeing their eyes flash with tenderness and sweetness...

Listening to her sorrow, holding her hand, hugging her close, and crying with her as she speaks of her pain...

Knowing what it feels like to have my heart overflow with compassion and love and understanding for God's children.

To all my friends, and all the lonely people I don't know, *yet,* I love you!

Postscript

For Carlotta, on our 12th Wedding Anniversary

Dearest: I give you the original script of this play of old sorrow, written in tears and blood. A sadly inappropriate gift, it would seem for a day celebrating happiness. But you will understand. I mean it as a tribute to your love and tenderness which gave me the faith in love that enabled me to face my dead at last and write this play — write it with deep pity and understanding and forgiveness for all the four haunted Tyrones.

These twelve years, Beloved One, have been a journey into light — into love. You know my gratitude.

And my Love! GENE

— Eugene O'Neill's dedication to *A Long Day's Journey into Night*

THIS BOOK has helped to heal me — and my family. After I wrote the chapter "My Double Calamity," I read it to my ex-wife over the phone. I broke down and sobbed all the way through my reading of it. I could hear her crying on the other end, and I could barely go on, choked up as I was. I hung up afterward saying, "This is all I can handle tonight. I love you, Kati."

Then I began to sob my heart out uncontrollably. My tears have moistened these pages for all eternity.

Acknowledgments

I SENT OUT some early chapters to a few friends. I was encouraged enough to widen the circle to more friends. The reactions were favorable, and I continued.

My girlfriend at the time told me — "for my own protection" — that I shouldn't show anyone else the book because it was full of bitterness, anger, and self-pity. It sent me into one of the worst downward spirals of my life. I was up the whole night, talking to my daughter, mother, and a few friends, trying to find a way to ease the pain. My friends urged me to plow ahead. I believed this story was much bigger than my hurt, or me, so I continued, slowly and with much nervousness and trepidation.

The writing of this book is exactly what my Chinese feng shui masters predicted: as I learned to trust a higher power, I would start to reveal myself. I began with baby steps, seeking encouragement every step of the way. The encouragement came and I opened up some more — until one day I knew I didn't need support anymore. I had learned to trust a higher power, and I knew I was protected. My reward was to receive some of the most beautiful and deeply moving responses of my life. I was deeply humbled by them. I learned that the compassion of human nature is as wide and as deep as the universe.

The best part of this book was how people reacted to it and what I learned from them. Their comments made me think and explore new areas of emotion and feelings, as well as others that had been repressed for years. In a way, my old and new friends,

134

recent acquaintances, and others joined with me in the creative process. They and their responses to what I was attempting to write are an integral part of this book. I felt an outpouring of love, which moved me beyond words, and I wanted to share this with others. I could not have gone forward on this project without this love and encouragement.

With love and gratitude,

Kiril Sokoloff

Of Related Interest

Henri J. M. Nouwen
LIFE OF THE BELOVED
Spiritual Living in a Secular World

Over 200,000 copies in print!

"One day while walking on Columbus Avenue in New York City, Fred turned to me and said, 'Why don't you write something about the spiritual life for me and my friends?'

"Fred's question became more than the intriguing suggestion of a young New York intellectual. It became the plea that arose on all sides — wherever I was open to hear it. And, in the end, it became for me the most pertinent and the most urgent of all demands: 'Speak to us about God.'"

— From the prologue

"Gentle and searching. This Crossroad book is a spiritual primer for anyone seeking God."

— The Other Side

Henri Nouwen is considered one of the great spiritual writers of our day. He taught at Harvard, Yale, and Notre Dame, and spent the last ten years of his life at L'Arche Daybreak community for physically and mentally challenged people in Toronto.

0-8245-1986-8, $14.95 paperback

crossroad

Of Related Interest

Wesley Granberg-Michaelson
LEADERSHIP FROM INSIDE OUT
Spirituality and Organizational Change

"There are three reasons why you should read this book. First, it is one of the clearest summaries you're likely to find anywhere of the best books and ideas about leadership available today. Second, it takes that knowledge a significant step deeper into wisdom; this is not just about the skills of leadership, but the spirituality of leadership. Third, it is written by an actual leader, not just somebody with thoughts about leadership."

— Jim Wallis, author and activist

0-8245-2137-4 $19.95 paperback

crossroad